SING O BARREN

Sarah Morgan

xulon
PRESS

Sing O Barren
by Sarah Morgan

Printed in the United States of America

ISBN 978-1-60477-710-9

Unless otherwise indicated, Bible quotations are taken from The King James Version of the Bible.

www.xulonpress.com

Sincere appreciation to my Vision International Family for your faithfulness, loyalty, dedication and your prayers especially in the year of the Lord's perfection 2007.

Thank you for standing with me. I love you ....dangerously!

Dedication

This book is dedicated to Deborah Abigail Morgan
An end-time prophetic voice.
Always remember, the song confronts the barrenness!

Love Mommy

Foreword

A man asked me recently when it was that I started writing down my messages. I told him it was about four years ago. My principal ascension gift is that of an evangelist. For many years, as a proclaimer and a declarer, I would get behind the pulpit, read one sentence and then preach for an hour out of that one sentence. If you didn't know the Word, you would just have to catch up with me. I would be quoting the Scriptures out of my belly, but then I realized that as God graduates us and takes us to other degrees He matures and settles us.

God began to teach me the importance and significance of tabulation in order to document the messages. I came to understand that I needed to have it all tabulated and written down in an archive whereby I could pull it out at any time as a reference point. This was one of the things that motivated me, and I learned from my husband Bishop Peter Morgan, that this work is forever.

I believe in leaving a legacy for the next generation, because, even when your natural voice has been silenced, your voice will still be heard through books. We are still being edified today from the patriots of old because what God gave them was put in writing. God told Moses something and said to write it down. In Revelation 21:5, He told John the revelator, *Write: for these words are true and faithful.*

If someone had not taken the time to write the Bible, we would have no reference point concerning the God we serve, so it is important for us to write. Whenever God gives you a thought, write it down. You never know when that thought will be a blessing to someone. If

God gives you a poem, write it down. If God gives you a song, write it down. You never know what will become of it in the future.

In the seventh month of the year 2007 the Spirit of the Lord began to speak to me, and I said, "Okay, God, I believe this is the season for me to release the fullness of this message from the book of Isaiah." So we are excited about this series "Sing, O Barren."

Isaiah, the son of Amoz, was a major prophet in that God used him to write a lengthy prophetic word in regard to the Messiah's coming, which is the promise of redemption for the nation of Israel. Here we see the account of Isaiah, speaking a perpetual covenant of peace to the children of Israel, and he encourages them to sing, O barren.

In this series we will be dealing with seven barren women as prototypes. Out of these barren wombs God has birthed or is birthing and releasing seven kingdom principles. Everything God does is for a purpose. God does not do anything without a divine purpose, and when we study the Word of God, when we tap into the realm of God, we begin to expand our understanding, knowing there is nothing God allows or nothing God does that is without a purpose that is not beneficial to His kingdom.

Part 1

Sarah

¹Sing, O barren, thou that didst not bear; break forth into singing, and cry aloud, thou that didst not travail with child: for more are the children of the desolate than the children of the married wife, saith the Lord. ²Enlarge the place of thy tent, and let them stretch forth the curtains of thine habitations: spare not, lengthen thy cords, and strengthen thy stakes; ³For thou shalt break forth on the right hand and on the left; and thy seed shall inherit the Gentiles, and make the desolate cities to be inhabited.—Isaiah 54:1-3

Through barrenness God births a kingdom principle. Each and every barren womb in the Bible had an assignment to birth a kingdom principle, to birth something into the body of Christ. The Lord is adjusting us in order that He might birth His will and His kingdom in the earth realm. In this book we will deal with seven barren women and seven barren wombs that conceived and birthed seven kingdom principles.

The word *barren* literally means to be infertile, to be sterile, to be unbearing, unfruitful and unproductive. In other words, God is saying, "I have wombs that are unproductive, but the reason I have allowed them to be unproductive is that through Me they will become productive and birth something significant in the earth realm and in My kingdom."

We're going to discuss Sarah, the first barren womb, that birthed Isaac, which means laughter, then Rebekah, Rachel, Manoah's wife, Hannah, Elizabeth and Mary. Each and every one of these wombs birthed a kingdom principle. Sarah birthed Isaac, which symbolizes laughter. Rebekah birthed Jacob, which symbolizes the principle of transformation. Until we have a transformation we are not qualified to bring forth nations. Rachel was the womb that brought forth Joseph, and Joseph birthed the principle of patience and humility. Manoah's wife birthed Samson, which signifies the birthing of an anointing and strength. Hannah birthed Samuel, which speaks of the birthing of intercession and the prophetic. Elizabeth birthed John the Baptist, which symbolizes preparation, repentance and purging, and Mary birthed Jesus, which symbolizes purpose and perfection. So out of these prototypes we will see seven principles that are released into the body of Christ.

I want to call to your attention from the reading in Isaiah 54:1-3 three things that caught my attention. The first was *sing*. What God is saying is that, if only you can open your mouth and sing, something is going to happen. In other words, God is saying we don't sing only when we're happy, and we don't sing only when we're rejoicing. We don't only sing when things are going well. God is just saying it's a kingdom principle for us to sing. When we sing we activate something in the realm of the Spirit.

The second thing that caught my attention is that something is going to happen when we sing. What is going to happen? We are going to break forth. He commands us to sing; then He commands us to break forth; and then He says to cry aloud. In other words, when we sing don't sing softly. We have to sing **loud**. When we sing loud, we break forth.

This is not just thinking a song; it is opening the mouth. It is about releasing something. The tongue is a creative force. When you open your mouth and sing you are crying aloud. Five things immediately happen when you open your mouth and sing, break forth and cry aloud.

The first of the five things that happen when you do this is you become enlarged. He said enlargement will come. The second thing that will happen will be a stretching. The third thing will be boldness. The fourth will be a lengthening, and the fifth will be a strengthening. These are the five things that will immediately start happening in your life, in your mind, in your heart and in your spirit when you start singing.

- **1. Enlargement**. In other words, the Christ in us, the God in us, is going to get bigger, and there will be an increased capacity to accommodate more. God can never give us more until we make room for more.
- **2. Stretching**. Your faith will be stretched. You are going to step out as never before. You are going to do things you thought you would never be able to do because God is going to stretch your faith. In other words, you will have more than you've ever had. You will give more than you've ever given because even your finances will be stretched. Jesus said to the man with the withered hand, "Stretch forth thine hand." In other words, you will do what you couldn't do before.
- **3. Boldness**. There is a spirit of boldness that is going to come upon you. There is a baptism of boldness. We have the baptism of the Holy Spirit; we have the baptism by water; but we also have a baptism of boldness (Acts 4:31). The Bible makes us understand there is a whole other message in the book of Acts that as the disciples were going out, they were persecuted and threatened by the people. The Bible says they went back into the room and they began to pray, and when they prayed the room shook with the power of the Holy Ghost and they were baptized with boldness. God is saying there is a boldness that is going to come upon you, that there is no demon, no witch, no wizard, no warlock, no sorcerer that is going to be able to intimidate you.
- **4 and 5. Lengthening and Strengthening.** In the midst of this there is a twofold promise.
  - a. The twofold promise is present, and it is future. There is a promise that God is going to activate presently (or immediately) and one futuristically. God wants us to

sing, and when we sing, the promise He is releasing will be immediately activated into our lives. Which is the ability to break forth on the right hand and on the left.

When you are singing, God is saying that you are going to explode. Your business is going to explode. Your vision is going to explode. Your ministry is going to explode, both spiritually and numerically, he is going to enlarge your territory.

b. Futuristically, God is promising that when you sing, your seed, your posterity; your children shall inherit the nations and make the desolate cities to be inhabited.

The first kind of barrenness is of God. The second kind of barrenness is of man, I will explain that in a minute. There are two kinds of people reading this right now. The first ones are those who have only heard *sing*. The second ones are those who have only heard *barren*. They say, "How can I sing because I'm barren? I'm unfruitful, I've tried everything. My business, everything that is going wrong—I'm just messed up. I'm barren." The barrenness that is of God is what God allows because He has a purpose He wants to fulfill through this barrenness. The barrenness that is of man is because of his belief system. He believes within himself that God can never change things, but the devil is a liar.

Sing is God's focus. *Barren* is man's focus. When God says, "Sing," that's the God-zone. The *barren* is man's focal point. God is not focused on *barren*; God is focused on the solution through the barrenness. The solution to the barrenness is to open your mouth and sing. So many of God's people are focused on their lack of fruit, and they are also upset about it. God wants us to open our mouths and have spontaneous songs of praise, when we are barren, unfruitful, infertile or unproductive; God is saying the solution to our barrenness is to *sing*.

There is somebody saying, "How can I sing the Lord's song in a strange land?" God is saying it's when we're in the season of barrenness, when we are in the season of unfruitfulness, of unproductivity, of lack and insufficiency, that we need to open our mouths by faith and sing. For without faith it is impossible to please God (Hebrews 11:6), and there's a comfort in the belief that He is the rewarder of them that diligently seek Him. In other words, you cannot tap into God's zone without faith.

Inspite of your circumstances, you've got to be able to open your mouth and sing because when you sing you create the substance, the undergirding, or the upper strata you need to elevate yourself into the realm of faith and begin to believe God for the miracle and the transformation.

God is not asking you and me to ignore the facts. He doesn't operate like that. Please understand. Faith does not ignore the facts. The situation is what it is. The teaching of faith has been going on so long that people can make you walk in this kooky, spooky realm of faith whereby you are almost in a place of denial. You say you're not sick, but yet you know you *are* sick. If you're sick, you're sick. If you're broke, you're broke, which is a temporary shortage of funds, But the Word says, *"but my God shall supply all my needs according to His riches in glory"* (Philippians 4:19).

It is pseudo humility. To say that you've got money when you don't have any. Or when you say,"by faith I'm giving this check," and you have insufficient funds to meet it. Please don't do that. God is not asking you to ignore the facts. He is just saying *sing* over it. In other words: I acknowledge I'm sick; I acknowledge I'm going through a bad season; I acknowledge I'm going through a barren time; I acknowledge I don't have money right now, but I'm going to *sing* over my barren situation. I'm going to *sing* over my barren situation so that God will initiate a change. I will just *sing* over it so God will initiate a change.

Returning to Sarah, being 90 years old, from a medical and biological stand point, It was absolutely impossible for her to produce a child, but God wanted to birth a kingdom principle through her barrenness. As you continue to progress in this book I will teach you that women in the Bible are symbolic of the church. This was the state of the church at one point. The church was barren. It took the power of God, and the act of faith, which is the currency of the Spirit. For the church which is the bride of Christ to be delivered from the spirit of barrenness.

God was trying to teach a principle through the life of Abraham and Sarah. In other words, God was saying to Sarah that even though you are 90 years old, when you begin to sing I will activate the cells in your body, reverse the menopause and cause your dead womb to ovulate and conceive. Like many of us Sarah laughed. Why? She laughed in unbelief because she could not believe God was able to turn around a situation that had been dead for the longest time. Know that God is the Alpha and Omega, the Beginning and the End, the One who has the power to raise anything because He created everything.

(1): In order for you to birth the principle of laughter, you must start *singing* before you see any fruit. Laughter is coming to the body of Christ. Laughter is going to be released. Laughter is going to be birthed in the body of Christ in the church. Literally God is saying that before you see the manifestation *start singing*.

Jesus made a very powerful statement in John 20:29: *"Blessed are they that have not seen, and yet have believed."* Why? Because when you are walking according to God's way (according to God's precepts) you walk by faith and not by sight. In other words, faith literally is believing God for what He has said. I haven't seen the manifestation, but I believe God. And as long as God has said it, it shall come to pass. I may not see it right now, but I know that, if God has spoken it, it will surely come into manifestation. If you are believing God for something, **sing**! If you haven't got it yet just open your mouth and **sing**!

So principle one is that you must start singing before you see any fruit. It's easy to complain when there is no fruit. It's easy to murmur when there is no fruit. It's not easy to sing when there is no fruit. Believe me, I know that but somewhere between the sighing and the song, there has to be some sight. God, when? How? Why me? When is it going to happen for me? When is my time coming? When is my season coming? When is my breakthrough coming? When is my miracle coming? When is my healing coming? All of that is in the realm of sighing. And God is saying that between the sigh and the song there has to be sight. In other words, sight is the ability to see in the realm of the Spirit. Once you see in the realm of the Spirit it will activate and energize you to call those things that be not as if they are. People will be asking what is it that makes you so confident to do what you're doing. What makes you so confident to stand the way you are standing? It's because you see what they don't see. In other words, "I already see my miracle, but I'm just waiting for the outward manifestation. I already see my breakthrough, but I'm just waiting for the physical manifestation. I already see my healing, but I'm just waiting for the physical manifestation."

(2): Sing, and you will break forth. When you open your mouth and sing, something happens in your spiritual womb, and that is conception. The power of song has been given to us to confront barrenness. The song of the Lord pushes back the darkness and introduces the light. As we sing we come into agreement with the song of the Lord. So no matter what is going on, as long as I open my mouth and sing, something is activated in my spiritual womb, and instantly conception begins to take place.

Then there is a forming that takes place which prepares me to birth what God has promised me. When we sing we challenge barrenness; we challenge unfruitfulness with the attitude of the Lord. It means I'm going to do something I've never done before, and that should be your mindset. That should be your belief system—when you're opening your mouth to sing and you know this has never been done before—and you believe God.

We're talking about Sarah. How could a 90 year-old woman bring forth a child? How could a hundred-year-old man? In the natural and in the physical it's absolutely impossible. God is saying that which is seemingly impossible in the realm of the natural is something that will surely come to pass in the spiritual realm.

In other words: I'm positioning myself to do something I've never done before, to say something I've never said before, to go to a realm I've never been to before. Nothing happens until you step out and you *sing*. In other words, it's not going to help you if you sit down and moan and murmur and complain about your situation. The more you murmur and complain and the more you have a pity party, the worse that situation will become. If I were you I would pass into God's zone, and instead of murmuring and complaining and talking about how it is never happening, open your mouth and *sing* and see what God will do.

17

Nothing happens until you step out. You can never step out until you *sing*. It is an act of faith for you to sing while you're going through something. It is not easy for you to *sing* when you're sick and your body is in pain. It is not easy for you to *sing* when you have an eviction notice and you've got just 24 hours to leave and find another place. I'm talking about unfruitfulness and unproductivity. It's not easy for you to *sing* when your business has not been booming the way you want it to. Your clients have not been coming the way you've been expecting them to come. It is not easy for you to pull out a song, instead it's easier for you to sit down and feel sorry for yourself.

So listen to me carefully. When you sing you are now shifting your focus from individuals and placing it on God for your breakthrough. You see, Sarah had to come to a place where she had to open her mouth in her barrenness and unproductivity and sing.

I've been barren, and I've been unproductive and infertile for so long. I have to get to a place whereby I shift my focus from the gynecologist and the doctors who have told me so many things and given me so many things and they still didn't work. I have to shift my focus now to the One who has the power to make it happen. See — all this time I had my focus on doctors, and the doctors couldn't do it. The preacher couldn't do it. So what do I do? I *sing,* and then I'll get God's attention!

Exodus 23:23-26 God speaks to His children saying:

23 *"For My Angel will go before you and bring you in to the Amorites and the Hittites and the Perizzites and the Canaanites and the Hivites and the Jebusites; and I will cut them off.* 24 *You shall not bow down to their gods, nor serve them, nor do according to their works; but you shall utterly overthrow them and completely break down their sacred pillars."*

In other words, all the stuff you've been depending on, all the stuff you've been looking to for your breakthrough, God is saying you're going to have to cut that out. And then He goes on in verse 25,

25 "So you shall serve the Lord your God and He will bless your bread and your water. And I will take sickness away from the midst of you. 26No one shall suffer miscarriage or be barren in your land; I will fulfill the number of your days." In other words, God is saying, "Remove your focus from the stuff, the people, the individuals, the system that you have depended on, and turn your focus on Me and begin to sing; then I will bless your food and your water, and you will no longer miscarry; and barrenness will be removed from you completely."

In other words, "Shift your focus to Me,"

The Bible says in Deuteronomy 7:12-15:

12 "Then it shall come to pass, because you listen to these judgments, and keep and do them, that the Lord your God will keep with you the covenant and the mercy which He swore to your fathers. 13And He will love you and bless you and multiply you; He will also bless the fruit of your womb and the fruit of your land, your grain and your new wine and your oil, the increase of your cattle and the offspring of your flock, in the land of which He swore to your fathers to give you. 14You shall be blessed above all peoples; there shall not be a male or female barren among you or among your livestock. 15And the Lord will take away from you all sickness, and will afflict you with none of the terrible diseases of Egypt which you have known, but will lay them on all those who hate you."

In 2 Kings 2:19-22 we read:

19 "And the men of the city said unto Elisha, Behold, I pray thee, the situation of this city is pleasant, as my lord seeth:

but the water is naught, and the ground barren. [20]*And he said, Bring me a new cruse, and put salt therein. And they brought it to him.* [21]*And he went forth unto the spring of the waters, and cast the salt in there, and said, Thus saith the Lord, I have healed these waters; there shall not be from thence any more death or barren land.* [22]*So the waters were healed unto this day, according to the saying of Elisha which he spake."*

The ground is barren because the city has a form, but what you see is not what it actually is. It looks a certain way, but the undercurrent of its spirit is not what you think. And that's the reason, even when you walk into church buildings, you shouldn't be impressed only by the decor. Check the spirit: know the spirit by the Spirit. That's why many people are in trouble today. They walk into a big city like Los Angeles where the lights are bright (the City of Angels) and everything looks nice. The buildings are beautiful, but an undercurrent runs through the city. If you do not discern the spirit and are just focused on the buildings, you will become a victim.

Basically what is happening here is that the water is bad and the land is barren. So what God is actually saying is, if your water is bad, something is happening tin the spirit around you, and if the ground is barren, find a prophet.

When you find a prophetic voice, the prophetic voice will give you the Word of the Lord. When the prophetic voice gives you the Word of the Lord, it will give you instructions to change something. In other words, the only thing that will cause the water to become good and the land to become fruitful is to do something new. Get a new level of prayer, worship and giving.

Why are most people barren, unfruitful and infertile?

2 Peter 1:5-9:

[5]*"But also for this very reason, giving all diligence, add to your faith virtue, to virtue knowledge,* [6]*to knowledge self-control, to self-control perseverance, to perseverance godliness,* [7]*to godliness brotherly kindness, and to brotherly*

kindness love. [8] For if these things are yours and abound, you will be neither barren nor unfruitful in the knowledge of our Lord Jesus Christ."

In other words, God is giving us the remedy that will break our unproductivity. If these things be in us, if these virtues are added to our faith, every barrenness in our lives, every infertility, every unproductivity in our lives will be broken. Continuing with verse 9, the Bible says:

"For he who lacks these things is shortsighted, even to blindness, and has forgotten that he was cleansed from his old sins."

It's not only a question of barrenness and unfruitfulness, but when we lack these things we are shortsighted. We have no vision. We cannot see farther than our noses.

This is one of the reasons the body of Christ, the church, is barren: because we have not implemented and added these virtues to our faith. And if we can only add these virtues to our faith, we will find that God will begin to activate and release the spirit of productivity in our lives. The word *barrenness* has two meanings. The first meaning is a Greek word that comes from *steiros* (which derives the English word "sterile") and means: to be stiff, to be hard or to be firm or obstinate. A lot of times we are sterile.,stiff. Hardheaded and obstinate. We are stubborn and stuck in our ways.

A closed womb is a closed mind, and a closed mind is a closed mouth. In other words, the main reason the church is barren and unfruitful is that the church has taken a stand in its thinking. It's set in its ways. "I refuse to change. This is the way I've always done it, and this is the way I'm going to do it. Nobody is going to change this. My granddaddy did it like this, and my daddy did it like this, and so I'm going to do it like this."

God trying to give us something that would change our situations and bring us out of a place of barrenness to a place of fruitfulness; but we're stiff-necked. And the reason this happens is that we are close-minded. When our wombs are closed, our minds are closed.

21

Why? Because our minds are the engine. Our minds are the focal point. Our minds are the headquarters and the processing center that generates the knowledge we need to make ourselves productive.

Being barren means having a closed mind, meaning I'm closed; I'm hard; I'm tight; I'm obstinate; I'm just not going to change. This is prevalent in the body of Christ. Please understand, if you are not teachable you are not reachable. If you think you already know, then you can never learn. It is hard to teach somebody who thinks he knows it all. I'm trying to give you the solution to your situation, but you've set in your mind that this is the way it is. "I refuse to open my mind. I refuse to open my spirit. So just leave me alone. Let me die the way I am."

"This is the theory I was taught. This is the principle I was taught. This is the way they taught me, and so I refuse to change." But if tthe way we've been taught is unproductive, and we've been going around the same mountain for forty years and have not seen a change. God is saying, "I want to renew your mind," if you open up, become flexible and allow me.

Please understand that every generation brings something new. The Word is the same, but the delivery is different because you're dealing with a different generation. You can't come into this generation preaching the message of the gospel in the manner or approach that my mother used to use. Why, because this is a different dispensation. Therefore the need to be open in order to receive what God has.

There are places in our thinking, in our belief systems, that are barren today, areas that are filled with unbelief. And God is saying, "Sing." It is difficult to deal with stubborn people. I have a policy. If I come to you once or twice and I discern that you're stubborn, difficult tp deal with, you'll never hear my voice again. Why? Because you think you know and yet I'm trying to help you get out of the place of barrenness and infertility so that you can begin to flow in the realm of productivity. But since you're set in your ways and that's the way your mother did it, that's the way your family does it, then keep doing it your way. When you get ready for a change, come and see me. *Sing!*

The second Greek word for *barrenness* is **Argos**, and it means not to work. It means to be inactive, to be lazy, to be slow. In other words, *barren* not only means sterile, as in stubborn, obstinate or set in your ways; it also means "won't work." "I refuse to work. I'm just lazy." A lot of people are unproductive because they just refuse to work. "I don't want to work. I'm just going to let manna fall from heaven because God said it." But beloved, God is saying it doesn't work like that. Someone said to me that the secret of success is found in four little letters W.O.R.K. 2thes 3:10 declares *He that does not work will not eat.* God demands us to work and do something in order to activate the blessing. Jesus said in Mark 3:5 to the man, *"Stretch forth your hand."* In other words The man with the withered hand had to do something before the miracle was activated. However, in order for you and me to work effectively, we must be filled with the Spirit of God to be fruitful. People are barren because they won't change and they won't work. They won't let God change them or work through them.

God was birthing a kingdom principle through the barren womb of Sarah.

Gen 11:30:

"But Sarai was barren; she had no child."

I want you to notice the spelling, *S-A-R-A-I.* Gen 17:15-16:

15 "Then God said to Abraham"—notice it's not Abram, but Abraham—"'As for Sarai your wife, you shall not call her name Sarai, but Sarah shall be her name. 16And I will bless her and also give you a son by her; then I will bless her, and she shall be a mother of nations; kings of peoples shall be from her.'"

Please understand. Laughter—Isaac—was not birthed out of Sarai. Sarai did not bring forth Isaac. Why? Because Sarai had a situation, and before you can birth the principles of God, there must be a change in your name and a change in your nature. God wants

23

to change and transform a part of you that is barren so you can enter into the realm of productivity. It's that part of you, the old nature, that is totally unproductive. God is saying, "I want to change your old nature and give you a new nature, because the new nature is the God nature that has the power to produce the principles of God for the kingdom."

Sarai means dominating, bitter and contentious. That was what *Sarai* meant. I want you to look at it from the standpoint of the church. There was a church that was dominating, contentious, bitter, manipulative, and that church was not productive. People went to church every week, and they left the way they came. There was no productivity; there was no fruit of the Spirit; there was no growth; there was no increase; there was no change in character; there was no change in behavior; there was no change in attitude. It was fruitless. Why? Because it was a church; it was a forum; it was a building, but it was *Sarai.*

God said, "As long as you are dominating, contentious, bitter and manipulative, I cannot produce a righteous seed out of you. There has to be a change of name and nature before I can release my seed into you to make you productive."

Sarah means a female noble, a lady, a princess or a queen. In other words, *Sarah* is a type of the church. What was once a domineering thing in the church is being turned into something noble and queenly. God is saying that church, *Sarai*—the church that was once stiff, rigid, inactive, lazy, religious, traditional and refusing to change and wouldn't work—is now changing to *Sarah* and is being transformed into a noble, queenly body.

"*Awake, awake...O Zion; put on thy beautiful garments,*" says Isaiah 52:1. Before laughter—Isaac—is born or released or birthed into your life, there has to be a change of name and nature. Isaac—laughter—was born to *Sarah,* not to *Sarai.*

Through the course of this book we are going to see the numerous changes of names and natures before we see the workings of God in the lives of individuals. God cannot use you in your old nature, in your old set in ways, stiff-necked obstinate, stubborn ways. He's got to change your nature, and that's the reason, when you are born again, there is regeneration. Your spirit is reconciled unto God. He brings you out of darkness into His marvelous light. Why? Because He changes you from the old nature to the new nature before He can release His divine seed into your spiritual womb for you to conceive and begin to bring forth the fruit of the kingdom. When God puts His nature in us, we are changed in name and nature.

2 Cor 5:17:

Therefore, if an man be in Christ, he is a new creature; old things are passed away; behold, all things are become new.

Laughter is ready to be birthed in your life. The principle of laughter is being birthed in the kingdom. The principle of laughter is being birthed in the church that has changed in name and nature. It is no longer dominating; it is no longer controlling. Control is witchcraft. In the past it has been a church that has not operated by the Spirit of God, but by another spirit. The Bible says in 2Corinthians 3:17 *where the Spirit of the Lord is, there is liberty,* and God is saying, "I am changing that, and as I am changing that, you will begin to see productivity coming. You are going to see the birthing of My qualities, My nature, My character and My gifts in the changed renewed church.

I don't know about you, but I hear laughter in the church and in my spirit. Before you can understand the concept of the principle that God is getting ready to birth which is laughter you have to understand what it symbolizes. Laughter is the symbol of conquest. Why does God sit in heaven and laugh? Because He cannot think of an enemy He has not conquered. Get ready to laugh and get ready to conquer your enemies. (Psalm2:4)

Even when the Bible speaks about the adversary, it is not God's adversary. God says it's your adversary. Your adversary is walking around seeking whom he may devour. First Peter 5:8 declares that the devil is your adversary. Revelation 12:12 says, "*Woe to the inhabitants of the earth...For the devil has come down to you*"—you, not God.

Also in Romans 8:37 the bible says I am more than a conqueror inChrist Jesus. Why because laughter is about to be birthed in my life, my family, my church, the body of Christ and overall in the Kingdom of God.

Isaac means laughter. *Isaac* means joy, but God wants you to know a change is coming. *Isaac* is coming. Conquest is coming. Victory is coming. Triumph is being birthed. Even though the Lord gave me this book, when I went back and revisited the material, something in my spirit leapt and rejoiced. Something in my spirit was activated, and I felt the laughter, victory, triumph; I felt the joy; I just felt something—the exuberance of God in my spirit. And I decree that laughter is being born now in our lives by the power of the Holy Spirit as God begins to change and transform our minds and our spirits and our belief systems.

Father, You are bringing us out of the place of **Sarai** *into* **Sarah**, *so that we may conceive the seed, which is the Word of God, and we would be able to break forth that which has the power to conquer our enemies.*

Now Sarah, our prototype, was in a place where she was saying, "God, I'm old."

But God was saying, "**Sing!**"

God, I already hit menopause."

God was saying, "**Sing!**"

God, I have no more feelings."

God was saying, even though you have no feelings, **sing!**

In Genesis 18 the Bible says that Sarah received a word from the Lord; likewise you are going to hear a word from the Lord today, and the word the Lord is speaking to you is this: "Is there anything too hard for the Lord?" And some of you will say within yourselves as you read this, "But, God, You don't know what I've been through. I've been barren a long time. I've been unproductive a long time. I've been infertile a long time. My business has not been productive a long time. My ministry is not flourishing. It's not working,. God. You don't understand what I'm going through. I've borne the shame, the reproach, the scorn, the embarrassment of barrenness. But God is saying sing anyway.

Can you imagine what Sarah went through when she got to a point whereby she felt, "I've been walking like a dead woman. I'm bitter because everyone else has had children but me. Everyone has succeeded but me. Everyone is prospering but me."

But she heard the Word of the Lord, and the Word of the Lord was this: "Is there anything too hard for Me?"

I don't know when and I don't know where, but between Genesis 18 and Genesis 20 something happened. I believe the death process in the womb of Sarah was not only stopped, but it was reversed and her womb revived. I decree and declare that the death process in your spiritual womb, your productivity, the place where God has ordained for you to be fruitful and multiply, be stopped and reversed in the Name of Jesus.

When I read this in the Word, the Spirit of God came on me and I began to cry because it ministered to me first. It was so deep that I got off my bed and fell on the floor and began to weep, because it was such a *rhema* word for me. It doesn't matter how unproductive, how unfruitful, how barren or how infertile your spiritual womb or your physical womb has been, something is going to happen because nothing is too hard for the Lord.

Genesis 21:1-5:

1 "And the Lord visited Sarah as He had said, and the Lord did for Sarah as He had spoken. 2For Sarah conceived and bore Abraham a son in his old age, at the set time of which God had spoken to him. 3And Abraham called the name of his son who was born to him"—whom Sarah bore to him—"Isaac—which means laughter. 4Then Abraham circumcised his son Isaac when he was eight days old"—Eight is the number of new beginnings. God is not only going to birth laughter, but something new—new ideas, new strategies, new schemes, new ways of doing things"—as God had commanded him. 5Now Abraham was one hundred years old when his son Isaac was born to him." Now I don't know how old you are, but if God did it for Abraham He will surely do it for you. 6"And Sarah said, 'God has made me laugh, and all who hear will laugh with me.'"

What she's saying is, "He has caused me to laugh, and all those who will hear of what God has done will no longer laugh at me." You know, people will laugh at you when you're going through your season of barrenness and infertility and unproductivity, when things seem as if they are not working for you.

Oh, it's easy for people to laugh at you and mock you and mock your God. They say, "aha, aha, where is your God now?" And if you say that your God is alive, "Then why are you barren? Why are you infertile? Why are you not productive? Why is your business not producing? Why isn't your ministry growing?"

God is saying that all who will hear will no longer laugh at you, but they will have no choice but to join in and laugh with you.

And in verse 7 this is what she said:

'Who would have said to Abraham that Sarah should have given children suck? For I have born him a son in his old age.'"–

–going back to the church as a type of the barren Sarah It is now in the latter days of the church that the true church is birthing sonship. I'm talking about true sonship in the Spirit realm. The former church was not able to birth because it was rigid, stiff, obstinate, and set in its ways, whereby God could not birth sonship through it." That is why we have a body that is full of crippled people. But as Abraham was circumcised (the cutting away of his fore skin) at the age of 99, then gave birth to Isaac his son at the age of 100, and as Sarah 's womb was revived at the age of 90 and by faith conceived and brought forth a son, so shall it be concerning the church in these latter days.

Laughter is being birthed. The first principle God is birthing in the body of Christ is the principle of laughter, which is symbolic of conquest. God wants us to walk not only as a conqueror, but also in the realm of more than a conqueror.

When I win this battle right here and I'm able to overcome this, that just makes me a conqueror; but when I can go over and beyond and bring that down, that's what makes me *more than* a conqueror.

I'm saying to you that in the same way God visited Sarah, if He ever promised you anything,, He will surely bring it to pass and will visit you also.

This is your hour of visitation; get ready to receive your promise.

Part 2

Sarah—The Reasoning Test

¹Sing, O barren, thou that didst not bear; break forth into singing, and cry aloud, thou that didst not travail with child: for more are the children of the desolate than the children of the married wife, saith the Lord. ²Enlarge the place of thy tent, and let them stretch forth the curtains of thine habitations: spare not, lengthen thy cords, and strengthen thy stakes; ³for thou shalt break forth on the right hand and on the left; and thy seed shall inherit the Gentiles, and make the desolate cities to be inhabited.—Isaiah 54:1-3

God wants to break the bands of barrenness, and He wants each and every one of us to come into the place of fruitfulness. God wants us to be fruitful. That was the first blessing God decreed on Adam and Eve.

Genesis 1:28:

And God blessed them, and God said unto them, Be fruitful, and multiply, and replenish the earth, and subdue it: and have dominion over the fish of the sea, and over the fowl of the air, and over every living thing that moveth upon the earth.

So you see here your beginning was a blessing. The word blessing means endowed to prosper; endowed to succeed. God is a God of covenant. The first covenant God cut with man was the seven-fold edenic covenant. The first of the seven edenic blessings to man was be fruitful. So here we see evidently that it is the will of God for each and every one of us to be fruitful. Iit is important that you keep that in your spirit as you continue to read. We are discussing in this book seven barren women God used to birth seven kingdom principles. We understand that God used Sarah to birth Isaac, or laughter, which is symbolic of conquest, and the womb of Rebekah God used to birth Jacob, which means transformation; the womb of Rachel God used to birth Joseph, which is the principle of patience and humility; Manoah's wife birthed Samson, which is symbolic of anointing and strength; Hannah birthed Samuel, which means intercession and prophecy; Elizabeth birthed John the Baptist, which was symbolic of preparation, repentance and purging; and Mary birthed Jesus, which was symbolic of purpose and perfection.

We have talked about Sarah at length, but before we move on to Rebekah, I'd like to discuss Sarah a little longer, as God has shed more insight as I continued to search the Scriptures. Everything God does is geared toward one thing, that Christ and the nature. of God will be birthed in you and me.

We go to church, we clap our hands, we sing, we have wonderful services, but the whole purpose, the whole endeavor of meeting together, breaking bread together and sharing the Word of God is that Christ, the nature of God, and the anointing, will be birthed in each and every one of us. When Zion travailed, she brought forth. So when you see a people, a church, a body that is travailing, it is travailing because there is a birthing. Travailing is always associated with birthing. So everything that is going on is geared toward birthing the nature of Christ in you and me.

The apostle Paul, in writing to the Galatian church, said, *"My little children, of whom I travail in birth again until Christ be formed in you"* (Galatians 4:19). He's not travailing that a gift will be formed in you; it's not about a gift. The gifts that are given to you dictate your potential, but your character, the God-nature that is being developed and formed inside of you, will take a travailing and a laboring. That's the reason Jesus said the fields are white unto harvest, but the laborers are few.

There is a difference between church people and laborers. Even at the level of leadership you have leaders who are laborers, and you have leaders who are just leaders, because labor entails a great deal of energy. Labor means you are going to have to sweat, and most people don't like to sweat. When God speaks about laborers He's speaking about people who are getting ready (or are ready) to put their hands to the plow and not look back.

Every time I stand before the congregation I stand as a laborer. I'm not standing there just so I can sound good. I am forming and creating something in the lives of my audience with my words. I am birthing. I am travailing that Christ will be formed in you. It's the law of duplication and rebirthing. Jesus said in John 6:63:

> It is the spirit that quickeneth; the flesh profiteth nothing: the words that I speak unto you, they are spirit, and they are life.

When Jesus was training the twelve He labored that His nature would be birthed in them. Therefore, when Jesus was taken away the twelve were still able to shake the city. As a matter of fact, they were not only able to shake the city, but they were also able to shake the world to the point that they went into a city and the people were calling them *"the men that have turned the world upside down"* (Acts 17:6).

What I am saying is that when the Word of the Lord is coming forth it's about birthing the nature of Christ in you. God is not so much concerned about your gifting as He is concerned about your character. That is why disciples are not made in three weeks. I just want to make that clear. God does not entrust real power with "flaky" people. The reason you are asked to come to church and to class on time is because this is the first step of responsibility and account-ability. If you can't be trusted to be at your class on time, how can you be trusted with power to shake the world?

Consistency is the key. You must be consistent in what you are doing because God is developing you and He is building in you a firm foundation. One of the problems we have in the church today is that many people are half-baked, not fully mature. The church is suffering because we have people who never ever finish the course. They get halfway through, and they feel they have it. What they don't realize is that they won't actually graduate until they pass the class.

Christ, the nature of God, is being birthed inside of you. One of the reasons I'm able to do what I do—and I know it's purely by the grace of God—is because of the grace of being consistent. I have never missed a Bible study. I have only missed a class because I was extremely sick or when I was pregnant and had just given birth or I am away on a Kingdom assignment.

Still, some come and finish the class, but they don't continue. John 8:31:

> *Then said Jesus to those Jews which believed on him, If ye* **continue** *in my word, then are ye my disciples indeed;*

Acts 2:42:

> *And they* **continued** *stedfastly in the apostles' doctrine and fellowship, and in breaking of bread, and in prayers.*

It is good for you to keep coming back. We need to be refreshed every now and again. Just sit back and listen to the teacher so God will continue to refresh you and you will be able to keep flowing in what God has given you.

There are seven things resident in you and me and the body of Christ that must be birthed. God wants that which is resident to become president in us. But before that can happen there has to be a change of our name and our nature. Before the birthing of a kingdom quality or principle there has to be a change in name and nature.

In the course of these seven barren wombs we are going to see the constant changing of names and natures. Jacob had to change from Jacob to become Israel before God would even release him to birth a nation. God can never use you effectively until you have changed your name and your nature. You've got to put off the old man and put on the new man because you can't put new wine into old wineskins. The new wine is fresh, vibrant and powerful, and if your wineskin is old the new wine will burst the skin.

So before we move on to Rebekah I would like to say that barrenness is a school or a class. It's good we are barren at some time. It is good sometimes that we are not fruitful. Why? Because God will teach us profitable lessons in those seasons. I n Psalm 119:71 David said, *"It is good for me that I have been afflicted; that I might learn thy statutes."*

The Test of Reasoning

Affliction is a school. Sometimes God will allow you to go through the school of affliction because He wants you to learn a lesson that will be beneficial to you and to your destiny. So please understand: **barrenness is a school.**

As with most tests the reasoning test has multiple choice solutions that are often masked in partial truth and then complicated by human error. You cannot reason God because God will show up in a way you don't even expect. You may be thinking God is going to fight with swords. When David went to face Goliath, he said in

1Samuel 17:45, 46:

"You come to me with a sword, with a spear, and with a javelin. But I come to you in the name of the Lord of hosts."

Now how do you fathom that? He didn't say, "I come *with* the name...." In other words, if I come *with* the name, the name is side by side with me. But if I come *in* the name, I'm literally covered by the name of the Lord God.

"But I come to you in the name of the Lord of hosts, the God of the armies of Israel, whom you have defied. 46This day the Lord will deliver you into my hand, and I will strike you and take your head from you. And this day I will give the carcasses of the camp of the Philistines to the birds of the air

and the wild beasts of the earth, that all the earth may know that there is a God in Israel."

You cannot explain, you cannot fathom and you **cannot** reason God. God is just God. People are always trying to analyze God. This is one of the issues we have and one of the things the apostle Paul had to deal with. When Paul got the revelation he picked it up in Romans 12:1-2. He had to go on his knees and beg them. He said:

1 "I beseech you therefore, brethren, by the mercies of God, that you present your bodies a living sacrifice, holy, acceptable to God, which is your reasonable service. 2And do not be conformed to this world, but be transformed by the renewing of your mind, that you may prove what is that good and acceptable and perfect will of God."

In other words, I beg you, by the mercies of God, that you be not conformed to the ways and to the systems of this world. Don't be conformed to the reasoning and the analytical answers that you think of for your solution, but be transformed by the renewing of your mind. Stop trying to figure out God.

The meaning of the word *reasoning* is the forming of judgments or trying to analyze. It also means logic, deduction, supposition, using reason for careful argument. Solomon picked it up in Ecclesiastes 11:5, where he said it is a mystery how a child is formed in the womb of a mother (paraphrase) just by the releasing of semen, blood is released and the body and bones are formed, and then a human being comes forth. It's a mystery. Stop trying to figure God out. God is just God.

Now we are going to deal with one of the major tests of barrenness, and that is the test of reasoning. The first thing I want to deal with is religious reasoning. In Genesis 16:2 we read: *"And Sarai said unto Abram."*

To reiterate,please understand, God cannot bring forth your miracle until there has been a change of name and a change of nature. *Sarai* did not birth Isaac. *Sarah* birthed Isaac. *Sarai* was renamed *Sarah* (which means a female noble or queen). *Sarah*, who had a new name and a new nature, is the womb that birthed Isaac. And *Abram* did not birth Isaac. It was *Abraham* that birthed Isaac. There had to be a changing of his name and his nature. At the age of one hundred he had to be circumcised (which means the cutting away of the flesh) before God could use his organ to release the seed of promise. So in order for *Abram* to become *Abraham* God had to breathe Himself into the name. And He said, "You have been Abram, but now I'm going to breathe into you my name and you will become **Ab-ra-ham** (which means the Father of the nations Genesis 17:5)." God changes your name and your nature before you can birth the promise of God.

Religious Reasoning

Genesis 16:2: *"And Sarai said unto Abram, 'Behold now, the Lord hath restrained me from bearing: I pray thee, go in unto my maid; it may be that I may obtain children by her.' And Abram **hearkened to the voice of Sarai**."*

This is *religious reasoning*. The difference between religion and relationship is this: when you are religious you are trying to find God your way; but when you have a relationship with Him you are not trying to find Him. He's found you! I already have a relationship with God, and because I have a relationship with Him I don't have a problem communicating with Him. I just simply believe what His Word says. But *Sarai* had a religious spirit, and when she realized they had a situation they thought could not be rectified she went to *Abram* with a religious reasoning. According to the New American Standard Bible, Sarai says, *"Now the Lord has prevented me from bearing children."*

Have you ever heard people who are sick and on the bed of affliction when you visit them make comments like "It is the will of God for me to be sick." The devil is a liar! That's a religious statement, because the Bible does not say God wills for you to be sick. The Bible says God is willing to heal all. He wants to heal you. It is not the will of God for you to be sick and afflicted.

You go into these places where people have a religious mindset, and they are reasoning from a religious standpoint. They say, "Well, I think it is the will of God for me to be sick so my life will be glorified through my sickness." How can God be glorified through sickness? What testimony can you have? The Bible says everywhere Jesus went everyone who touched Him was healed, **all of them**. They were all set free, all delivered. Jesus healed everybody! Acts 10:38 declares:

> *How God anointed **Jesus** of Nazareth with the Holy Ghost and with power: who **went about doing** good, and healing all that were oppressed of the devil; for God was with him.*

Where did you get this reasoning? It's partially right and partially wrong. But the partial truth Sarah walked in became the basis for spiritual error. Anytime you begin to reason religiously, you are destined to fall into error. One of the greatest obstacles to your miracle, is the reasoning factor. Why? Because my circumstances do not match up with what God said. God said one thing, but my circumstances are saying another thing.

What happens is that you begin to reason with yourself, and God is saying, "You've got to stop reasoning, because you cannot fathom who I AM. And as high as the heavens are, so are My ways." (Isaiah 55: 8-9) It's a question of having faith in God and having hope in God. Having hope in God (not in your circumstances). God will never change. The Lord had not prevented Sarai from having children forever, but religious reasoning made her think that was it. You've got to be able to match up what you are saying with what the Word of God says.

Did God say He wants you to be barren? No. The Bible says to be fruitful and multiply, replenish the earth and use the vast resources of the earth (Genisis 1:28). If God didn't say it, what makes you think that is the will of God for your life? Don't make permanent decisions over a temporary situation. Just because it looks bad right now doesn't mean it's going to *stay* bad. (Your present situation is not your final destination.) All I need is a little time, and as you continue to walk with God trusting in Him and believe what His Word says, God is going to turn my captivity.

The Bible says the Lord turned the captivity of Job. And when He turned the captivity of Job He gave him double for his trouble. Job 42:10 says;

And the LORD turned the captivity of Job, when he prayed for his friends: also the LORD gave Job twice as much as he had before.

You see, we have a tendency to put a period on our lives where God has only put a comma.When people looked at Job they thought Job was going to stay in that situation forever. When his wife came she was using religious reasoning. She said, "Why don't you curse God and die, because I don't see you ever coming out of this? This is it, Job!" And Job said, "How can I do that? I must uphold my integrity." In other words, he would rather die trusting God than live doubting God. The enemy puts you into that place of religious reasoning. But it was not God's plan. If God said it, then God would do it because God is not a man that He should lie (Numbers 24); neither is He the son of man that He should repent. So then the question is: Did God say it?

If God said it, it doesn't matter how long it takes. All I know is that in the furtherance of time, it shall come to pass. Why? Because I believe God. A delay is not a conclusion to the matter. It was a case of divine timing. Religious reasoning caused *Sarai* to take the matter into her own hands and devise a plan for fulfilling God's promise through Hagar who birthed Ishmael.

God does not honor our religious remedies. When you slip into religious reasoning, it causes you to devise other means to fulfill what only God can fulfill. In other words, let us help God! God, You're not coming on time; so since You're delayed let me help You.

You don't have to do a thing to preserve the name and the integrity of God. God's name has its own integrity. He is God all by Himself. That's the reason He can sit down and boast. He said, "I AM God, and I sit upon the circle of the earth, and I behold the inhabitants of the earth as grasshoppers. I AM My own counselor. I AM Alpha and Omega. I AM the beginning and the end. I AM the Eternal, the

Immortal, the Invisible, the Only Wise God, the Ubiquitous One and the One that does not change. I AM God. There is nothing you can do or say that will change who I AM." Anything we do outside the will of God, God will never honor. When we start to put everything into our own hands, we devise our own means to help God.

For instance the Word of the Lord says in Proverbs 18:22:

*Whoso] findeth a wife findeth a **good thing**, and obtaineth favour of the LORD.*

So when you get a Word from the Lord that God is going to give you a husband your responsibility is to *become* a good thing. But then you start reasoning. That's when you want to do it your way. Hence you change your attire, you change the way you walk, when you see a brother in the church whom you like and then start making advances on him; it's called seduction. Even if it ends up in marriage, guess what? Because you didn't do it God's way, you birth and Ishmael. An Ishmael is going to be a problem not only to you, but to the world!

When Naomi began to prepare Ruth for her Boaz, she gave Ruth specific instructions (Ruth 3:3). She said, "Wash yourself, girl. Change your clothing." In other words, "upgrade the way you dress because you're getting ready to go to another level. Anoint yourself with some perfume. In other words, you've got to have some smell-good going on. Why? Because you're getting ready to come into a new realm and a new dimension that will cause you to walk in the fulfillment of the promise I gave you." This has both natural and spiritual connotations. It's not just about preparing your outward appearance, but also your inner man. You must be prepared both physically and spiritually.

Ruth obeyed the Naomi's instructions and counsel completely so when she went into the field of Boaz, which is a type of the church, she began to glean. She was just working. She didn't come looking for the husband. She just came to work and began doing the work of the Lord. She did not go into the field looking for Boaz. She went into the field doing the work Naomi had told her to do. When she went into the field and did what Naomi had told her to do, it was Boaz who spotted her. Because she had become a good thing. Likewise when our goal in the church and in the kingdom is to let the word of God wash us, change us, and anoint us, for the work of the ministry, when our focus is to please God first we will not need to look for our Boaz, rather he will find us.

Religious reasoning. God doesn't need help from you. The funny thing about religious reasoning is the tendency to take a little portion out of the Bible (but not the whole portion) and say, "Well, this is what the Word of God says!" Throw down the reasoning with your mind and with your intellect and get in the Spirit for God is a Spirit. (John 4:24) Your mind and your intellect do not touch God. It is your heart and your spirit that touches God.

When stuff is not working the way you want it to work, God is saying, "I told you, but because you went ahead of Me with your religious reasoning, you birthed an Ishmael." Ishmael is not God's will and He will not honor Ishmael. He may bless Ishmael to a certain level, but Ishmael is not the promise. You may see a little bit of blessing, but not the fullness of it, because you did it outside the will of God with your religious reasoning trying to help God.

Please understand. It was four thousand years after Adam and Eve sinned that God sent the remedy. In other words, God was moving according to His divine agenda and a divine itinerary. So when Adam and Eve disobeyed and ate from the tree God didn't stop moving. God did not interrupt His agenda to deal with them. He said, "I'm going to give you a temporary covering because I've got to keep moving, and when I finish with this cycle I'll come back to deal with you." And guess what happened? He didn't come back till four thousand years! (Read Galatians 4.) The Bible says in the fullness of time God sent His Son born of a virgin. For four thousand years people were waiting for the redemptive plan of God, and God was saying, "Nobody interrupts My agenda. Judgment is going to have to wait for the fullness of time. When I finalize everything I've scheduled to do, then I'll come back to you."

Point number one is *religious reasoning*. God does not honor our religious remedies. Stop trying to help God. God is big enough, and

He is more than able to do what He said He will do. Point number two is the *good-source reasoning*.

Go back again to Genesis 16:2b. So Sarai said to Abram, "*See now, the Lord has restrained me from bearing children.*" See—that's the *religious reasoning*. The religious mind always makes it look like it's from God. Remember Naomi? When she left Bethlehem-Judah? God didn't tell her to leave. People have a tendency to do stuff based on their own intuition, and then they blame God when things go wrong. "Don't call me Naomi; call me Mara for the Lord hath smitten me." No, God didn't smite her. She smote herself when she left Bethlehem-Judah (the house of bread and praise) and went down to Moab.

Good-Source Reasoning

This is now Sarai speaking to Abram, continuing in Genesis 16:2: "*So Sarai said to Abram, 'See now, the Lord has restrained me from bearing children. Please, go in to my maid; perhaps I shall obtain children by her.' And Abram heeded the voice of Sarai.*" This illustrates point number two—the *good-source reasoning*: when you are reasoning from a good source. Why was it a good source? Because Sarai was the one that was barren. Sarai's voice was influential in this matter because she was the suffering barren woman and she was the beloved wife of Abram. You need to watch the sounds that come out of the person who is the victim: "You see, you don't know what I'm going through. If you were in my shoes, you wouldn't be saying what you're saying. If only you knew what I'm going through, you'd probably be saying the same thing I'm saying." And that was the level of influence her voice had because she was the victim in this case. When a person is the victim, then the voice is very strong and very influential because it makes you feel compassion. And Sarai said, "There is something you can do to help me. Go into Hagar, my maid, and lie with her so that she can conceive and have a son for me." But the reason it was so powerful was that she was the one who was suffering. The sound of her voice brought a sense of assurance and security. Surely God would honor what this suffering, frustrated, humble woman of God desired.

I say it all the time. God is not a sentimental God. My daughter will ask me, "Mom, what do you mean by that?" I stand on what I believe because I have the evidence that God did not even spare His Son, and that is the highest level of sacrifice. There is no father who would see his son die and not move in to rescue him, but the Bible is clear: God spared not His Son!

In Isaiah 53:10 the Bible says, *"For it pleased the Father to bruise the Son."* Now what kind of father is that who would be pleased to bruise his son? What am I saying? God is not so much a sentimental God as a principled God. God is no respecter of persons. He is a respecter of principles! To the point that even when Jesus was in the Garden of Gethsemane, the Bible says, He looked up and said, "If it be possible, remove this cup from Me." That was Jesus in His humanity, but in His divinity he said, "Nevertheless not My will but Thy will be done." When Jesus was going through that pain, as a father God could have come down immediately and said, "My Son, I feel Your pain. Let Me relieve You from this." But no. God in His sovereignty and deity did not. and He reminded Him (Jesus) that for this purpose He came. Which reminds us that the only time we are pleasing in God's sight is when we walk in the fulfillment of the purpose God has sent us to...(at all times).

So the good-source reasoning can be very influential and persuasive. After all, God had been silent concerning the issue; therefore, it is our responsibility to carry on. We say, "I've been praying and fasting, and I haven't heard from God." So we start our own reasoning. No, if God does not say anything just *sit down* and **wait**. **Wait** until your time comes.

Do you remember when King Saul was waiting for Samuel to come to offer a sacrifice unto the Lord (1Sam 7)? Samuel represented the prophetic voice. They were waiting for him to offer the sacrifice to the Lord, but Samuel was delayed. So Saul said to the people, since they had everything they needed for the sacrifice (the animals and the bullocks), that they should offer this sacrifice to God and God would be pleased. But that was the influential sound. Saul was a king and not a priest, and because he was king the people hearkened to the influence of his voice. They acted when it was not right since they thought Samuel was not coming, for the duties of offering sacrifices to the Lord were for the priest.

Please understand: delayed is not denied! Just because God did not come when you wanted Him doesn't mean He isn't coming. The Bible says when Samuel showed up he saw the smoke and the sacrifice and said, "What have you done?" Saul said, (paraphrase)"Well, we just thought because you were late we would help you, and since we are sacrificing to God, God would be pleased. But it was not so.!"

Now then the reasoning factor regarding Abram's response to the influence of Sarai resulted in the birthing of Ishmael whose offspring would be a thorn in Israel's side for generations. Not only a thorn in the side of Israel, but also a thorn in the side of the world. A lot of what we are experiencing now, the hostility between Islam and Christianity, including the threats of terrorism, are a direct result of the sons of Ishmael, because they were not born according to the will of God. They are the sons born from the bondwoman. Why? Because of the reasoning factor that was going on when God was trying to teach the *faith factor*.

Cultural Reasoning

The third point we're going to deal with is: ***cultural reasoning***. We are still talking about barrenness (Genesis 16:1). *"Now Sarai, Abram's wife, had borne him no children. And she had an Egyptian maidservant whose name was Hagar."* Sarai had within her household an answer to her problem. In your house you have a plan B. That is **not** absolute faith, because when you are walking in absolute faith you don't need a plan B because you take God at His word. But in her house Sarai had a plan B. In other words, in case God did not come through she had her plan — plan B.

If you believe in God for a hundred thousand dollars, you say, "I'm believing You, Father, and in the name of Jesus I pray that You will release the money for the project I have." But somewhere in the back of your mind you already have a plan B in case God doesn't come through; That is not walking by faith. Like most of us, Plan B for Sarai was right there in her house, and that was Hagar, an Egyptian maid. What she proposed was a common practice in those days for the purpose of procreation and continuity of the family name. It was an acceptable cultural practice to handle what seemingly could not be changed: barrenness. So Sarai thought her situation would never change; and according to their pagan culture, if a wife was unable to bear children, then it was okay for her husband to get another woman to carry his seed. That was part of the Egyptian culture.

This is still part of the African culture today. If you get married and there is no child for four, five, six years, then those influential voices begin to speak into your head. What's going on? It is unheard of that there is no seed coming! Mr. So-and-So down the street has a young, blossoming daughter I think would be wonderful. After all, the two of you have nothing going on; it's just so that your name can continue. But how many of you know that whomsoever you join yourself to, you become **one** with? It doesn't matter who it is. The Bible says in the book of 1 Corinthians 6:16 that "*he which is joined to an harlot is one body.*" And that's the reason you need to be careful about whom you lie with. After you lie with someone an exchange takes place, and after that exchange takes place you'll wonder why a particular spirit keeps following you. Why? Because you pick up something when you lie with something. There's an old saying that goes, "If you lie down with dogs, you'll get up with fleas." And you just thought you were going over there to have a nice time and then leave. Oh, no! It's deeper than that and that's why you need to be careful what you do.

Many times people have gotten into situations in which they are fine until they lie with somebody. But that person they lie with has a history. So they were not only lying down with the opposite sex but with everything else that person had lain with. So when you lie with a person and suddenly stuff begins to happen and you start wondering, "What's going on with me?"

People think it's just that simple. But the Bible says that whoever you lie with you become **one** with. That's the mystery of godliness. It says *the two shall become one.* So when you lie with an individual you take on the spirit of that individual. It doesn't matter who you are, you do not have the strength unless God helps you.

Some of you are wondering why you keep feeling some sexual proclivities and inclinations, why you keep gravitating to them. You keep going back even though you don't want to be there, but something is pulling you there. Why? Because when you left you picked up something. You didn't leave by yourself; you left with a spirit, and it became a soul tie—and it's going to take the power of God and the power of deliverance to *set you free*. People think it's that simple, whereby you just lie with her so your family name will continue. It is not so. No, no, no! Something happens! And that's why Sarai had a problem with Hagar.

When Abram lay with Hagar and brought forth Ishmael, at a certain point Ishmael grew and began to mock Isaac. Why? Because technically speaking Hagar felt she had established a right as a wife, because she had carried Abrams seed and birthed his first son. Now, women, you know what I'm talking about. Once you get that connection, then suddenly you think you are in charge.

Now Sarai is looking at this maid who used to respect, help, and serve her, and now her attitude has changed. Something is going on. In other words, Sarai had given away her power and postition so that now the maid is on the same plane as Sarai. Sarai, by culture, had asked and proposed a common practice, because it was an acceptable practice to handle what seemingly could not be changed, which was barrenness. And Abram allowed the thoughts, patterns and practices he had learned from the pagan culture to influence his thinking.

Many times, when we come into the kingdom, we bring some tendencies and practices with us from our cultures that are locked into our belief systems. Christianity is the epitome of all cultures. So you cannot serve God according to your culture.

When we come into the Kingdom, we conform to its culture. You need to understand that's why Paul said, "I beg you that you be transformed by the renewing of your mind.(Romans 12:1) "Why? Because you are coming into a whole new culture which is the kingdom culture. You cannot bring the philosophies and ideologies from your culture and home into the Kingdom; it would serve as a conflict of interest.

Remember the woman at the well? That was an issue right there, because Jesus was now trying to bring to her attention a new focus and emphasis of worship. In other words, it is not **how** or **where** you worship; it is **whom** you worship. The woman at the well was culturally caught up with the issue of worship according to the tradition of the Samaritans. Hence making her rigid, stagnant and inflexible as a result of not being able to make a connection with God. Likewise we too can serve a problem when we come to the church and attempt to serve God based on our traditions and cultures, consequently hindering the spirit of God from moving as He wills as a result we do not receive our breakthroughs, blessings and healing.

2 Corinthians 3:17:

*"Now the Lord is that **Spirit**: and **where** the **Spirit** of the Lord is, there is liberty."*

The Bible says the ark of Moses was more or less a sitting ark. In the book of Amos, chapter 9, verse 11, God says He will raise up the tabernacle of David which was a spontaneous tabernacle (mobile). In other words, no longer would you bring the sacrifice of goats and turtle doves and pigeons, but now you will bring the sacrifice of praise, which is the fruit of your lips. So then what is God saying? God is saying that when you come into Him you are no longer worshiping from a stagnate place. You are now a moving tabernacle, and the way His Spirit moves is where you move; how His Spirit moves is how you move.

Roman 8:14:

*For as many as are **led** by the **Spirit** of God, they are the sons of God.*

So you can't just come in and be stiff when everybody is praising God and worshiping and lifting their hands because of your tradition. Loosen up and enjoy the presence of the Lord.

Abram allowed the patterns and practices he had learned from his pagan culture to influence his thinking, but God wanted *Abraham* and *Sarah* to use faith before God could move in their circumstance,, not **Hagar:** the *cultural reasoning* answer. Faith is the God answer; Hagar is a *cultural* answer. The *cultural* answer is your means of trying to do what only God can do, and God is saying, "No, I don't want you to do that. I want you to birth something that I respond to: and that is called **faith**." Please remember—the father of faith was Abraham but the author and initiator of faith is God. Because God had impregnated Abraham with the seed of faith He had to take him through the process in order for Abraham to birth **faith**. God was teaching him a principle: that he would not be able to do it his way, for "*without faith, it is impossible to please God; and they that come to God must believe that He is a rewarder of them that diligently seek Him*" (Hebrews 11:6).

I'm trying to bring a point home. God is breaking barrenness in His church. No longer will you be unfruitful. God is saying, "Enlarge your faith. Stretch forth and fortify your faith, because I am doing something, and you must enlarge your capacity to accommodate what I'm getting ready to do." God is bringing in the harvest. I don't know about you, but I'm excited about what God is doing. The harvest is coming, and for some of you who are not ready, let me tell you, it's just going to come upon you suddenly. All of us at some point face the same dilemma, and when we face that dilemma what is challenged? Our ability to trust God's Word, God's way and God's simplicity, which at times can be mind-boggling. The *religious reasoning, good-source reasoning* and *cultural reasoning* may be some of the greatest obstacles we will face before God moves mightily in our lives and in our situations.

At times it is easier to follow our natural inclinations and cultural wisdom and use available resources in order to bring the blessing we so desperately need and desire. But God is saying, "That is not the way I want you to do it." Without faith, it is impossible to please God. Why? Because faith is the currency of the Spirit. It is the spiritual element God responds to. Anything we do outside of faith is Ishmael. Romans 14:23 says that "*whatever is not of faith is sin.*" The cultural context is both challenging and a source of temptation. We are to minister within our culture but not allow cultural methods and philosophy to replace the simplicity of our faith in God's Word and God's power.

Ephesians 3:20 says, *"Now to Him who is able to do exceeding abundantly above all that we ask or think, according to the power that works in us."* And what is the power that works in us? It is the power of faith.

Genesis 21:1 says, *"And the Lord visited Sarah as He had said, and the Lord did for Sarah as He had spoken."* At the set time she conceived. When God's visitation comes, it comes to refresh, to revive, to renew, to restore and to make alive again.

Shout! It is your hour of visitation. I decree and declare all things in your life are being revived, refreshed and renewed.

The Lord showed me something. He said, "The people out there in the world have a saying, Fake it till you make it." And the He said for me to tell you to change that. From now on it's "Faith it till you make it." When you are going through and you don't seem to see the breakthrough of God and people are asking you what's going on, all you have to do is look at them and say, "I'll just faith it till I make it."

And Abraham believed God and it was imputed unto him for righteousness (James 2:23). Romans 4:20 says that *Abraham did not waiver at God's promise*, but he was strong in faith, giving glory to God. Unbelief, doubt and staggering are products of a barren heart. In Psalm 78:19 and 2 Kings 7:2 we read how the people doubted God. They said, "Can God prepare a table in the *wilderness?*" It was a product of unbelief that caused them to stagger, even after everything God had done for them. He sent manna out of heaven and caused water to come out of a rock, and yet they came to a place where they staggered. God is saying unbelief, doubt and staggering are products of a barren heart.

This points us toward the problem of leaning on our reasoning tendencies. To stagger means to make use of our own judgments and rationale in discovering things. To stagger at the promise is to take into consideration the promise and all the difficulties that lay in the way of its accomplishment and to dispute its fulfillment. Staggering is not to cast it off fully nor embrace it fully, but to waver over it.

God is asking, "How long will you halt between two opinions?" (1 Kings 18:21). In other words, you don't fully disbelieve; but at the same time you don't fully believe, so you are just wavering between doubt and belief. That's what staggering is. God is saying we should not stagger, but be stable and stay focused because He who will come, will come, and He will not delay in the fullness of time.

Hebrews 10:37-38:

For yet a little while, and he that shall come will come, and will not tarry.
38 Now the just shall live by faith: but if [any man] draw back, my soul shall have no pleasure in him.

I said all that to say this: God wants to give you one message. While you are waiting for your womb to be opened, for your productivity to be stimulated and activated, you've got to pass the reasoning test. You cannot reason with God. God is not a man. God is above man, and therefore, that puts you in a place whereby you must surrender and give it all to God. Whatever you want to do, however you want to do it, whomever you want to do it with, your allegiance is to serve God. No matter what happens we must serve Him the rest of our days. Once you do that you give God permission to come in and work on your behalf.

When God says vengeance belongs to Him, the moment you take vengeance into your own hands, God steps back. He says, "Okay, if you think you can fight and you've got the muscle, go ahead." But when God says, "You will not need to fight in this battle, for the battle is not yours; it is Mine," He means it. In other words, back off and let God take charge of it, because it's bigger than you! It's bigger than your mind! It's bigger than your bank account! You can't fight it, but God is asking you to let Him handle it with His divine, supernatural muscles. Who can fight God and win? So whoever your enemies are they become God's enemies. One of the names of God is Jehovah-Elohim (the Eternal Creator). He is El-Gibbor (Man of war), a mighty warrior. *"Lift up your heads, O you gates; and be lifted up, you everlasting doors; and the king of glory shall come in"* (Psalm 24:7). He is the king of glory. He is the God of battles. He would never ever lose a battle. God is teaching a principle: what you can't do, let Him do!

I realize in my own life that I get to a point when I start trying to help God. And the moment I stop trying to help God, that's when God comes in. As a matter of fact, I get to a point sometimes when I'm praying and praying about a certain thing, but nothing is happening. And God says, "That's the whole problem right there, because you are thinking you can manipulate Me. And another thing you think I'm deaf." He may not talk to you like that but He talks to me like that. We have a relationship; I'm His child. And He tells me, "I heard you the first time!"

God is saying, "Don't stagger!" Say to yourself: I will not stagger. I will not give up. I will wait for the promise, and as I'm waiting I will sing. I will cry aloud. I will break forth until my visitation comes.

Part 3

Rebekah

1Sing, O barren, thou that didst not bear; break forth into singing, and cry aloud, thou that didst not travail with child: for more are the children of the desolate than the children of the married wife, saith the Lord. 2Enlarge the place of thy tent, and let them stretch forth the curtains of thine habitations: spare not, lengthen thy cords, and strengthen thy stakes; 3for thou shalt break forth on the right hand and on the left; and thy seed shall inherit the Gentiles, and make the desolate cities to be inhabited.—Isaiah 54:1-3

Now we are dealing with the second barren womb, which is the womb of Rebekah.

In Genesis 25:19-22:

19"And these are the generations of Isaac, Abraham's son: Abraham begat Isaac: 20And Isaac was forty years old when he took Rebekah to wife, the daughter of Bethuel the Syrian of Padanaram, the sister to Laban the Syrian. 21And Isaac intreated the Lord for his wife, because she was barren: and the Lord was intreated of him, and Rebekah his wife conceived. 22And the children struggled together within her; and she said, If it be so, why am I thus? And she went to enquire of the Lord."

As we saw earlier, there are seven things resident in you and me and the body of Christ that must be birthed. God wants that which is resident to become president in us. You will recall that the barren womb of Sarah brought forth Isaac, which means laughter, joy and strength and is symbolic of conquest. But before that could happen there had to be a change of name and nature. *Sarai* had to become *Sarah*, and *Abram* had to become *Abraham* before Isaac, the seed of promise, was brought forth. That's why we must be born again. We must be regenerated. "For that which is born of the flesh is flesh, and that which is born of the Spirit is Spirit" (John 3:6).

Isaiah 62:1-2:

1 "For Zion's sake will I not hold my peace, and for Jerusalem's sake I will not rest, until the righteousness thereof go forth as brightness, and the salvation thereof as a lamp that burneth. 2 And the Gentiles shall see thy righteousness, and all kings thy glory: and thou shalt be called by a new name which the mouth of the Lord shall name—and that name is Jesus."

When you are born again, when you are regenerated, when you are reconciled to your original status, God calls you by a new name, and that's the reason you cannot allow folks to mess up your day by calling you by your old name. As long as you have been washed in the blood of Jesus, you are no longer the person you used to be. People have a tendency to call you by your old name, even when you have been born again, filled with the Holy Spirit, water baptized and fire baptized, and yet every time they see you they have a tendency to call you by your old name and your old nature. They say, "Oh, are you talking about So-and-So, the junkie?" Or, "Do you mean Brother So-and-So, the addict?"

God says when you are regenerated He calls you "by a new name, which the mouth of the Lord shall name." So we are going to be dealing with the principle of transformation. From the barren womb of Rebekah, God birthed transformation. Remember: the **song** confronts your barrenness. As long as you have a song you are able to confront your barren situation, and God will bring you into the place of fruitfulness and abundance.

In Romans 12:1-2 the apostle Paul said, according to the Amplified Bible:

> *1 "I appeal to you therefore, brethren, and beg of you in view of all the mercies of God, to make a decisive dedication of your bodies as a living sacrifice, holy, devoted, consecrated, and well pleasing to God, which is your reasonable, rational, intelligent service and spiritual worship. 2And do not be conformed to this world"—in other words, to this age, fashioned after and adopted to its external superficial customs— "but be transformed"—changed— "by the renewing of your mind"—and in brackets it says, "by the new ideals and its new attitude"—"so that you may prove what is that good and acceptable and perfect will of God."*

In other words, the writer is saying we must be transformed by the renewing of our minds. God doesn't want us to get another mind. God is not looking for you to purchase another mind and replace the mind you have, because the prefix *re* means "again" or "anew." *Renew* means to make new again. The mind you already have needs to be renewed so you can be brought back to the mind you had in God before Adam fell. He is not looking for us to get *another* mind, just to *renew* the mind we already have.

When God created Adam He created him in God's image, after His likeness. In other words, Adam was the expression, the very likeness of God, in the earth realm. So when God named Adam and then Adam named the animals, Adam was just imitating what his Daddy did. So we had a mind in God that operated one hundred percent, and God is saying He desires us to renew our minds so we can come back to the mind we had in Him before we ever hit the earth, the mind that is able to name things so they stay named what we name them.

Your mind constitutes your will, thoughts and your emotions. It's your intellect and your psyche, which operate like a womb. The Spirit realm is the realm from which the seed comes: whether from God, man or the devil, It is then planted in the womb of your mind, and there conception takes place. Once that happens, then the process begins that develops the conception into thought. Then the thought begins to come through the birth canal of your speech—which is called words.

Your words are ambassadors of life and death. Your words look like you.

Proverbs 18:21:

Death and life [are] in the **power** *of the tongue: and they that love it shall eat the fruit thereof.*

Don't tell me you didn't mean it when you said it. Why? Because it took time to be impregnated and conceived in the womb of your mind, and it took time for whatever it was to be processed so it became a thought; then it came through the birth canal of your speech in the form of words. So when you released the words you meant what you said! I don't believe it when people say, "Well, I wasn't thinking when I said it." That is not true! How can you speak if you weren't thinking? Your words are processed within the thought realm in your mind. You *were* thinking. Why? Because your thoughts became words, and then your words became speech. Your words look like you, and that is why you need to watch the words that come out of your mouth. Your speech will always betray you.

When the Spirit of the Lord moved upon the face of the deep the Spirit technically did not have a voice. He was moving, but He was waiting for a voice to give Him direction. The words you speak determine the parameters in which the Spirit of God will go. So, until you speak, the Holy Ghost does not have direction. He is just Spirit. He is liquid. He is moving (hovering) until you give Him some kind of direction, until you give Him some kind of specific direction. Open your mouth and say it! Job 22:28.

*Thou shalt also **decree a thing**, and it shall be established unto thee: and the light shall shine upon thy ways.*

It wasn't until God **spoke** and said, "Let there be light," that there was light! You need to watch every idol word, every barren word that comes out of your mouth, because it will be brought to judgment. Therefore, I am saying a closed womb is a closed mind. A closed mind is a closed mouth. A closed mouth is a closed decree or declaration that can change your situation. The declaration precedes the manifestation. If you can say it, you can have it.

God has placed teachers and governors in the body of Christ, called the five-fold ministry (Ephesians 4:12), to show us, instruct us, guide us and give us principles to walk and live by. We all need someone to speak into our lives. Abraham sent Eliezer to find a bride for his son (Genesis 24), Isaac. Likewise, God has sent the five-fold ministry to find and propose a bride for His Son, Jesus.

Remember we are talking about the womb that birthed transformation. Transformation is getting ready to be birthed in the church, in your home, in your business. You are getting ready to see a transformation in every area of your life.

Be Willing

▪ (1); In order to birth transformation, you must be willing.

Genesis 24:58: *"And they called Rebekah, and said unto her, Wilt thou go with this man? And she said, I will go."* For you and me to birth transformation, we must be willing.

Those that would become impregnated with the fruit and the principle of change and transformation are those who are willing to follow Eliezer, a type of the Holy Spirit and a type of the five-fold ministry gifts. You have to submit to a voice of authority in your life. Until you and I come to a place of submission to a voice of authority, God is not going to do what He desires to do through us and in us. Therefore, we must be willing to follow; willing to obey; willing to submit; willing to listen; willing to take instruction. The Bible says Rebekah was willing. She was willing to follow Eliezer. She was willing to follow that which God had placed in her life. She was willing to follow the principal voice that was giving her instruction, which was taking her into her destiny and into her purpose.

A lot of us have missed destiny and purpose because we are not willing. In Isaiah 1:19 God declared that if we are willing and obedient we will eat the fruit of the land. In other words, God uses, and elevates willing people. We cannot do the work of God with an unwilling heart. So when God says to move, *move*. When God says to stand up, ***stand up***. When God says to sit down, ***sit down***. When God says it's time for a change, ***it's time for a change!*** When God says it's time to change your attitude, change your behavior, change the way you talk, then **do it!**

The Bible says Ruth was willing to follow Naomi before she came into her purpose and destiny. She said to Naomi, (paraphrase) "Entreat me; don't stop me from following you, because there is something in you, that is connected to my destiny. When we sense by the way of the Spirit that somebody has the key our next level, our destiny, and our purpose, we must be willing to follow until we come into the fullness of if.

Elisha was willing to follow Elijah. He said, "I will not turn back, man of God, because I sense by the Spirit that you are carrying in your loins my destiny and purpose (paraphrase). It doesn't matter how much you challenge me; I'm not turning back. Challenge me at Gilgal, Jericho, and Bethel; I refuse to turn back, until I receive a double portion of your spirit. **We must be willing!**

Make a Conscious Covenant

- (2): before you birth transformation you must make a conscious covenant. Genesis 24:60-61 the Bible says:

60 "And they blessed Rebekah, and said unto her, Thou art our sister, be thou the mother of thousands of millions, and let thy seed possess the gate of those which hate them. 61 And Rebekah arose, and her damsels, and they rode upon the camels, and followed the man: and the servant took Rebekah, and went his way."

Rebekah—whose name means "tethering" or "tying," symbolizing a rope or a noose, something that fastens—was a covenant woman. She was a woman who knew how to tie herself to what was able to take her into destiny and purpose. In other words, she wasn't playing games.

God doesn't use people who are not serious. God doesn't use halfway committed people. The church makes me laugh when they think they can just come and go as they please and think they can carry a mantle of power. I have news for you. One of the requirements to carry a mantle on our shoulders is the ability to be consistent and totally committed to the cause. It is only for people who are committed to the cause and who are ready to die for what they believe. But it's not for us until we are ready to die for it, until we are ready to come to a place where we say, "For God I live, and for God I die. It doesn't matter what comes my way. I have made a decision to follow Jesus."

We often sing the song in Sunday school, "I have decided to follow Jesus. No turning back, no turning back." In other words, we cannot be in God today and be in the world tomorrow. We cannot say we love Him today and then not know whether we love Him tomorrow! We cannot say we think we are saved today and then tomorrow vacillate in our spirits and not know if we are actually saved! The devil is a liar! We must be able to make a conscious decision.

In Psalm 89:34 God says, "*My covenant I will not break, nor alter the Word that has gone out of my lips.*" In other words, God is saying He is a God of covenant. He is a covenant-making and a covenant-keeping God. (A covenant is a permanent binding relationship). In other words, we must be committed.

There are two kinds of commitment

1. The first is **casual commitment**. We have a lot of people who are just casually committed. It's like a couple who are dating.

The woman is not looking for a casual affair; she is looking for a permanent commitment, but the brother is just looking for a casual fling. We must get to a point in our lives when we are not available for a fling. God does not get involved with us casually. We are either serious, or we are not. We are either doing this, or we are not. We are either going all the way, or we are not going at all. If we are not ready to say, "I do," or declare the "M-word" (marriage), then this relationship is not ready to take off.

Men and women of God, this is a tragedy with the church. We come into the church the same way we come into the world. We bring in the stuff we do in the world, and we bring it unto God. We have people coming into the church when all they want is a casual affair. All they want is to flirt with God. All they want is for God to make them feel good. They don't want the penetration. They don't want the seed of God which is the **Word**. They don't want to be impregnated. They don't want the responsibility of birthing and teaching and raising. They come to church just looking for a good time. This is how it is now with the hottest church in town! So the people can go there and have a wonderful time. The praise and worship is good. The singing is beautiful. The preaching is good and entertains the flesh and greases the ego. But fosters no commitment.

2. The second commitment is a *covenant commitment*, a serious, permanent commitment. Casual is not serious. Casual is not locked in. Casual is halfway in, halfway out. You can always tell when someone is just casual. He is wonderful in the early days when the candle has been lit and the atmosphere is dim. The conversation is fine until you start bringing in the question of permanent commitment. When you mention making a permanent commitment, his face changes and begins to twitch. Oh, no, he is not ready for that piece of paper. But the devil is a liar! The piece of paper means *we are committed.*

I have never seen anybody go to cut a deal with any major company where they are just "playing around." It's not a game!

When you are getting ready to handle some major bucks, do you think you are just going to deal with it in a casual way? No. You are going to have to sign some documents. You have to put your name on the dotted line. It may take you all day to sign on the dotted line, but you are going to sign so everyone will know you have made the commitment!

Casual is not serious, but a *covenant commitment* means you are willing to relinquish your name for another name. It means you are willing to walk down that aisle and say, "I do." It means you are willing to leave your people, leave your family, leave your house, your property, and make your people my people. And this was Ruth when she said, "I'm willing to make your God my God. Where you die, I will die. Where you go, I will go." This is a covenant—that your God, your beliefs, your persuasion I am willing to follow, and it shall become my persuasion. I am willing to leave and cleave because I am in covenant with you: for better, for worse, in sickness and in health, for richer, for poorer, till death do us part.

When we make a covenant with God, all we are, all we have, is His. In other words, the moment you merge, you are no longer your own. You can no longer do things the way you want to do them. Why? Because we are no longer two; we are one. So you cannot decide today you are going over here and I am going over there. No. We have to agree because we are no longer two; we have become one.

God is saying that before we can birth transformation, we must make a covenant commitment that we have chosen to follow this persuasion. This is the reason we cannot just make casual commitments to the church. We will never be a full partaker of the blessing (that is under the umbrella) until we are joined. As long as we are separated and having a casual relationship, you can have just so much from me or know just so much about me; but the moment we join, then I am liberated to give you all my stuff. You can have my bank account number; you can have all my stuff. Why? Because we are now joined. But if we are not joined you cannot have everything. There is another portion remaining. Jesus said He could not give the bread of the children to the dogs.

I preach everywhere the full counsel of God's Word, but when I minister at home there is a greater emphasis in regard to the delivery and impartation of the Word of God because it is the local body where I serve. The saints have made a covenant commitment to pay their tithes and offering that there may be meat in the storehouse as opposed to the universal body (Malachi 3:10-11). And that's another factor the body of Christ must take note of. You have no right to pay your tithes outside your local body that prays for you, feeds you, nourishes you and has oversight over your soul. If anything happens to you it is your local overseer that will be held accountable for your soul. If you have a death in your family it is your local pastor who officiates the funeral services. If you want to be married it's your local pastor that weds you. If you have babies it's your local pastor that dedicates your children.

When you make a covenant with God, everything that is His is yours, and everything that is yours is His. In other words, your life is His; your children are His; your marriage is His; your business is His; your ministry is His; your money is His. Your money does not even belong to you. It belongs to God.

Overcome the Roots of Pride

- **(3): pride.** Before you can birth transformation, you have to overcome the roots of pride. One of the keys to trans-formation is overcoming one's roots. Rebekah was a Syrian, which means "highland" or "exalted." One of our greatest obligations before being changed and birthing transformation is to remove the loftiness of pride. The carnal mind is the enemy of God. Anytime you exalt anything above the knowledge of God it is pride.

The Bible says God opposes pride. Pride is one of the reasons Lucifer was kicked out of heaven. Pride caused Lucifer, who was the morning star, to fall out of favor with God; therefore, God opposes pride. So when Satan infiltrates and invades the mind of men the first thing he plants there is pride. The same thing that got him kicked out of heaven is the same thing he uses to try and get you and I kicked out of the presence of God.

In 2 Corinthians 10:3-6

3 "For though we walk in the flesh, we do not war after the flesh: 4For the weapons of our warfare are not carnal, but mighty through God to the pulling down of strong holds; 5casting down imaginations, and every high thing that exalteth itself against the knowledge of God, and bringing into captivity every thought to the obedience of Christ; 6and having in a readiness to revenge all disobedience, when your obedience is fulfilled."

In dealing extensively with the spirit of pride in the *Ten Character Tests*, we saw that pride was one of the tests Joseph had to pass. It is literally the mystery of iniquity that emanates from the son of perdition. God tells us not to think higher of ourselves than we ought to. (Romans 12)

So Rebekah, who was a Syrian, had to overcome the pride of her roots before God would open her barren womb and she was able to conceive and bring forth transformation.

The Struggle

- (4): **the struggle**, because it is not easy to birth transformation. In

Genesis 25:22-27,

22 "And the children struggled together within her; and she said, If it be so, why am I thus? And she went to enquire of the Lord. 23And the Lord said unto her, Two nations are in thy womb, and two manner of people shall be separated from thy bowels; and the one people shall be stronger than the other people; and the elder shall serve the younger. 24And when her days to be delivered were fulfilled, behold, there were twins in her womb. 25And the first came out red, all over like a hairy garment; and they called his name Esau. 26And after that came his brother out, and his hand took hold on Esau's heel; and his name was called Jacob: and Isaac was threescore years old when she bare them. 27And the boys grew: and Esau was a cunning hunter, a man of the field; and Jacob was a plain man, dwelling in tents."

Before you and I can birth transformation, get ready for a struggle. The Bible says Rebekah asked the question, "If the Lord has heard my prayer, why the struggle? If I am walking in the will of God, I'm doing what is right, so why the struggle? God gave me a promise; He gave me a prophecy; but I don't understand why the struggle?" You know you are doing what is right. You are praying; you are fasting; you are seeking God. You are paying tithes, reading your Bible, doing everything you are supposed to do, and you are trying to live a righteous life. Then why the struggle?

There is a struggle going on in us because God is trying to birth transformation. God is trying to birth a change. Every time God is getting ready to birth change, there will be a struggle because people don't like to change. Birthing transformation is a struggle. It is not easy to change, and it is not easy to be transformed because we are set in our ways. How are we going to change the way we have been all our lives? Change the way we think? Change the way we behave? Change the way we deal with people? Change the way we talk? Transformation is not easy.

There will always be a struggle between **two nations and two natures**. Rebekah was carrying two nations and two natures in her womb, and therefore, there was a struggle going on in the womb of Rebekah. **You are going to experience a struggle between the God-nature and the man-nature** that is in you. You want to do what is right for God, but there is another law that is working in your members. Why is it that when I come out of an anointed service where the power of God was moving, people were saved, healed and delivered, the power of the enemy hits me the moment I leave the meeting? It's because there is a struggle going on.

David was a man of war. David was God's anointed. David was the apple of God's eye. David was the sweet psalmist of Israel. David was God's favorite. David's head was anointed with oil. David was a mighty warrior. David never lost a battle. How is it that David came from the frontline of a furious battle and in a matter of minutes was in a struggle of another kind? He was looking from the roof and saw a naked woman, and another nature kicked in. In spite of all the anointing, power and deliverance, yet there was a struggle.

There are two nations. two natures. There is a hairy man, full of iniquity like Adam; he is a mighty hunter but is interested in satisfying his appetites, gratifying his flesh, even at the cost of his inheritance. That is **Esau**. The Esau nature is in every one of us.

There is another nature in us which is a conniving, supplanting, lying nature which is Jacob. He too is in every one of us. As it was in the womb of Rebecca, so it is in every one of us, the struggle of these two natures. There were two natures fighting and struggling in the womb of Rebekah, and Rebekah asked, "If this be so, why the struggle? If You called me to serve You, why am I struggling? If You anointed me, why am I struggling?" In other words, why do I feel holy sometimes and feel like the devil at other times? Why do I feel spiritual one day and then carnal the next day? Why do I have my flesh under control one day, and the next day I'm looking to gratify my desires and the demands of my flesh at any cost?

It's because there are two natures and two nations struggling in us. Before we can birth transformation, there must be struggle. If you really want to birth transformation and be transformed to the place where you have prevailed with man, which is flesh, and with God, which is divine, there will be a struggle.

Galatians 5:17:

"For the flesh lusteth against the Spirit, and the Spirit against the flesh: and these are contrary to one another, so that you do not do the things that you wish."

There's a struggle going on. Why do you leave church after of a powerful service and go home and watch pornography? You came out of a powerful service; hands were laid on you; you thought you were delivered, but the moment you left the atmosphere of God, you stepped outside and lit up a joint! Why would you come out of an anointed environment and step into your car and sniff some cocaine? It's because there is a struggle going on. Why do you come out of prayer where you've fallen out in the presence of God and wept and cried, and then you step into your bedroom and masturbate? There is a struggle going on. The Spirit is lusting against the flesh, and the flesh is against the Spirit. You will strive, toil, labor, fight, battle, wrestle and contend because it's a struggle. between good and evil; between right and wrong; between flesh and Spirit; between darkness and light; between truth and error; between God and the world. Aren't you tired of the struggle?

If God said it, then why the struggle? It's because you are birthing transformation, which is not easy to birth. Even Jesus struggled with the flesh in the Garden of Gethsemane, and He said, "Father, if it be possible, remove this cup from Me. Nevertheless, not My will, but let Your will be done." In other words, there's a struggle going on. He's saying, "My flesh can't take the pain. I can't take what is about to happen to Me, but not My will; let Your will be done."

Paul said in Romans 7:18-24:

18"For I know that in me that is, in my flesh, dwelleth no good thing: for to will is present with me; but how to perform that which is good I find not. 19For the good that I would I do not: but the evil which I would not, that I do. 20Now if I do that I would not, it is no more I that do it, but sin that dwelleth in me. 21I find then a law, that, when I would do good, evil is present with me. 22For I delight in the law of God after the inward man: 23But I see another law in my members, warring against the law of my mind, and bringing me into captivity to the law of sin which is in my members. 24O wretched man that I am! Who shall deliver me from the body of this death?"

66

Transformation is of the mind, that you may be renewed and transformed by the renewing of your mind, your will, your intellect, your emotions, your desires and your lower nature. It has taken you prisoner to the law of sin which is in your members.

There was a struggle in Rebekah, but **Sing, O barren**, because the song confronts the barrenness. Jacob who will become Israel is coming forth. Travail, labor, push, because transformation is coming. Be transformed from a liar, a supplanter, a conniver to a prince who has prevailed with man and with God. In other words, there is another man, another woman, another generation in us that is coming out of you and out of me. A transformation is coming to your mind, to your marriage, to your family, to the church, your community and this nation.

I decree and declare a transformation in your attitude and in your behavior. I decree that your body is transformed from sickness to health, and your spirit from oppression to deliverance. **Sing, O barren!**

The church has been governed by the Jacob-nature for many years which is a supplanting, conniving and scheming spirit. But God is saying we are coming into a place where the womb of Rebekah is getting ready to birth the new move of God. No longer will we be in a position to connive, to scheme, to manipulate, to intimidate, but we will be able to stand in a new realm whereby we become the prince who has prevailed, both with God and with man. Glory!

The assurance that brings us into destiny and purpose is we know what God said. "Rebekah, you will be the mother of thousands, and your seed shall possess the gates of your enemies."

Wrestle

- (5): final test before we birth transformation is **the wrestling test**. Get ready for the wrestling match. Genesis 32:24-30:

24 "And Jacob was left alone; and there wrestled a man with him until the breaking of the day. 25And when he saw that he prevailed not against him, he touched the hollow of his thigh; and the hollow of Jacob's thigh was out of joint, as he wrestled with him. 26And he said, Let me go, for the day breaketh. And he said, I will not let thee go, except thou bless me. 27And he said unto him, What is thy name? And he said, Jacob. 28And he said, Thy name shall be called no more Jacob, but Israel: for as a prince hast thou power with God and with men, and hast prevailed. 29And Jacob asked him, and said, Tell me, I pray thee, thy name. And he said, Wherefore is it that thou dost ask after my name? And he blessed him there. 30And Jacob called the name of the place Peniel: for I have seen God face to face, and my life is preserved."

Many of you are going to establish your **Peniel,** because you will see God face to face, and your life will be preserved in Jesus' name.

My final key before you can birth transformation is that after you have struggled with yourself get ready to wrestle with God, because the struggle is within yourself. It is sin, another law that is working in your members. So you have a **struggle** within yourself, but after you have struggled with yourself get ready to **wrestle** with God.

The word *wrestle* means a contest between two in which each endeavors to throw the other, which is decided when the victor is able to hold his opponent down with his hand upon his neck. Jacob was left alone, and there wrestled a man with him. In other words, struggle is within yourself; wrestling is with God. When God wrestles with us, it's basically bringing us to the point of letting the best Man win. Who can fight God and win? If we have to come out of this fight with a limp we will birth transformation, and our names will be changed. We will no longer be called Jacob, which means thief, robber, supplanter, schemer, trickster, liar, but will be called Israel, because we have become a prince who has prevailed both with God and with man. God is saying that the day has broken. *Genesis 32:26, And He (God) said, "Let Me go, for the day breaks." But he (Jacob) said, I will not let You go unless You bless me!"*

Say, "God, I'm not letting You go until You bless me, until You change my name, until you change my nature. I will not let You go until You change my status." And the Bible says he prevailed. The word *prevail* means to overcome, to have power, to be able to gain or accomplish or endure or reach. God says, as you are birthing transformation, everything you were not able to do you will now be able to do. Everything you were not able to gain you are now able to gain.

Everything that was taken from you God says He is going to restore it to you. Why? Because you have prevailed with God and with man. You have prevailed with the divine, and you have prevailed over your flesh and are now transformed into another man. No longer is your name Jacob, but your name is now Israel. God says you will be able to endure, because when God changes your name He increases your endurance. In other words, it looks good, smells right but because I am no longer called Jacob, but Israel, I have endurance over my proclivities.

Because we have prevailed, our endurance has increased. So we overcome with the blood of the Lamb and with the word of our testimony. To prevail means to be a victor, to have ability and strength. When we prevail with God and with man, God brings us into the place of Ephesians 3:20: *20 "Now unto him that is able to do exceeding abundantly above all that we ask or think, according to the power that worketh in us."*

Today we have birthed transformation. He has given us a new name.

Say this prayer: *"I am a prince; I am an overcomer; I am victorious; I am more than a conqueror, and I can do all things through Christ who strengthens me. I am about to birth a generation that will birth generations and generations and generations because my seed will be like the stars in the heavens and the sandon the seashore. In Jesus' name, amen."*

Part 4

Rebekah—The Contradiction Factor

¹Sing, O barren, thou that didst not bear; break forth into singing, and cry aloud, thou that didst not travail with child: for more are the children of the desolate than the children of the married wife, saith the Lord. ²Enlarge the place of thy tent, and let them stretch forth the curtains of thine habitations: spare not, lengthen thy cords, and strengthen thy stakes; ³for thou shalt break forth on the right hand and on the left; and thy seed shall inherit the Gentiles, and make the desolate cities to be inhabited.—Isaiah 54:1-3

I truly believe the season of barrenness is coming to an end in the body of Christ. I believe we are coming into the season of fruitfulness, and God is dealing with everything that has caused us to be barren, unfruitful, sterile and infertile in the past. Why? Because God's desire for you and me is that we be fruitful and multiply.

Our key Scripture passage is Isaiah 54. We are dealing with the seven barren wombs God used to birth the seven kingdom principles. The womb of Rebekah was used to birth the principle of transformation, which was Jacob who became Israel. Now we will deal with Rebekah and the contradiction and the intercession test.

Genesis 24:60,

"And they blessed Rebekah, and said unto her, Thou art our sister, be thou the mother of thousands of millions, and let thy seed possess the gate of those which hate them." Another translation reads, "And let thy seed possess the gate of your enemies."

There is a spiritual law of contradiction that is seen all through Scripture, and at some point in our faith walk we must encounter this particular law of contradiction. Nobody is exempt from the law of contradiction. Hebrews 12:3:

"For consider him that endured such contradiction of sinners against himself."

Therefore, we understand that even Jesus had to deal with contradiction.

The definition of *contradiction* is: an opposition, to assert the opposite point of view, to speak in denial, to have someone oppose you. A contradiction is where things tend to be contrary to each other, a thing containing contradictory elements (in other words, what you have when your circumstances don't line up with God's promises).

There are several occasions in our walk with God when our circumstances have not lined up with the promises of God. We can even get to the point when everything around us is contrary to what God said about us and we say to God, "God, I don't even think I heard You." Most of God's servants who have received the promises, the vision, the dream of faith and direction were tested and challenged with this thing called *contradiction*. For example, Abraham and Sarah received the promise of a miracle son, but she was barren. Imagine how Sarah felt when God spoke to them and said their seed would be like the stars in the sky and the sand on the seashore knowing that she was barren **Contradiction!**

Joseph dreamed of promotion and prosperity but received imprisonment and hatred. God gave him a dream that he would be powerful, that he would be great, that his sheaves would stand up and the sheaves of his brethren would bow down to him, and the next thing that happened was Joseph ended up in prison and lies were being told about him. **Contradiction!**

Moses received the word he would be a deliverer but was rejected and sent into the wilderness. **Contradiction!**

God sent Samuel to anoint David as the next king of Israel, and automatically what comes to mind when you think kingship is a palace, a beautiful place, a beautiful room with people serving you. But the next thing you know, David is driven into the caves of Adullam and he's being chased like a fugitive. **Contradiction!**

God gives the vision, but where is the provision to meet the vision? The vision was clear, so why don't you have the finances? Why don't you have the resources? **Contradiction!**

God said the land the Israelites were going to was the land of milk and honey. (God was going to deliver them with a strong hand through the hand of Moses.) They ended up in the wilderness where there was no food and no water. **Contradiction!**

"Lord, You said I was going to be a millionaire, but I can't even find a job, let alone start a business." **Contradiction!**

"Lord, You said by Your stripes I was healed, and I am healed, but I still see the symptoms. What's going on, God?" **Contradiction!**

"I paid for my college education, and I got a degree and went on to get a master's degree, but still there is no company that wants to hire me." **Contradiction!**

Contradictions in life and ministry are numerous and are part of God's sovereign school of shaping greatness. Contradictions are our crosses, and we are commanded to bear them according to Matthew 16:24. God allows contradictions to test our responses or our reactions. In other words, He is saying, "I know what I told you, but I want to see what's in your heart. I want to know your motivation for what you are doing. I want to be sure you have the right heart, the right spirit, and the right mind before I release it to you."

It's a heart issue! How do you respond or react when your circumstances don't line up with the promise? This is where "the rubber meets the road." This is how you know what people are really made of. This is where you separate the sheep from the goats and the powerful from the weak. How do you handle the situation?

It is easy for us to say we have faith and we believe God and we know He is able to do exceeding abundantly above all that we ask of Him according to the power that works in us. It's easy to open our mouths and quote the Scriptures. *"But without faith, it is impossible to please God, for they that come to Him must believe that He is, and that He is a Rewarder of those who diligently seek Him"* (Hebrews 11:6).

However it isn't easy to keep on believing God when you are in a dire situation. You can have enough faith when it's one week and you may still have a little faith when the situation goes two weeks, but let it go to a month or six months! That's when everything, the good, the bad and the ugly, starts to happen. **Contradiction!**

It's all right when everything is wonderful! It's fine when you have money in the bank, but not if you are out of a job and the bills are piling up! To the child of God who is filled with the Holy Ghost and knows the Word of God, it is **Contradiction!**

When nothing is lining up with the Word of God, then what do you do? That's the measure right there! That's the plumbline! We have plenty of fair-weather Christians. When the going is good, everything is wonderful! When the going is good, they come to church; they clap their hands; they praise the Lord. But when the winds become contrary and blow in a different direction are they still going to stand and believe God? Will you be able to stand still until you see the salvation of God? How do you respond when your circumstances do not line up with the promise? Will you become bitter, better or broken? Will you become soft, or will you become hard?

In Isaiah 41:10 says,

"Fear thou not; for I am with thee: be not dismayed; for I am thy God: I will strengthen thee; yea, I will help thee; yea, I will uphold thee with the right hand of my righteous-ness." He will harden us to situations. In other words, our trials and challenges are designed to harden us to situations. The Amplified Bible says, "Fear not; there is nothing to fear, for I am with you; do not look around you in terror and be*

dismayed, for I am your God. I will strengthen and harden you to difficulties, yes, I will help you; yes, I will hold you up and retain you with My victorious right hand of rightness and justice."

God allows the **contradiction test** to test our responses. God allows *contradiction* to enter our perfect world: (1). to press us; (2). to break us; (3). to bring us to our knees. So that when we finally receive our breakthrough we will be able to say that day, "If it had not been for the Lord on my side, where would I be?"

You know, some people have a tendency, when everything is going wonderfully, to think it was by their might (and not by God's). They think they were able to do, achieve and attain everything because of their education, knowledge and their finances. So every now and again God will allow *contradictions* to mess up their perfect little lives.

In our season of *contradiction* our confession changes as we embrace the unchangeable circumstances of life. It may be a disease that refuses to let go of a friend or a loved one, an accident that takes a godly person into eternity at the height of his or her life, a church that splits right after a vision meeting or a church that grows numerically, financially and in other ways—while the senior pastor is living in sin! **Contradiction!**

Contradiction and affliction are the tests of all promises, dreams and visions, but it is only a test! Rebekah, Isaac's wife, received a promise of unparalleled growth and increase.

Genesis 24:60 they blessed Rebekah and said to her, *"Sister, may you become the mother of thousands and ten thousands and may your descendants possess the gates of your enemies."*

Rebekah, who birthed transformation, received the promise of: (1) divine blessing; (2) supernatural growth; and (3) victory in warfare. But everything around her was a **contradiction** to the promise and the blessing that was spoken on her life. How could she be blessed to be mother of thousands of ten thousands, to be victorious and an overcomer of her enemies and those who did not love her, discovering she was barren, unfruitful, sterile, infertile and living like a loser instead of a winner? **Contradiction!**

In Matthew 16:18-19 there is a promise given to the church: He (Jesus) will build His church, and the gates of hell shall not prevail against it—a powerful, apostolic, prophetic promise. You and I need to understand that no matter how powerful, no matter how great, the promises are that have been released into our lives, the test of barrenness is certain!

Times and seasons will arise when all we do is covered with barrenness rather than growth or prosperity. Three promises were given to barren Rebekah, and I want you to know God has given you a promise.The only thing that keeps me standing, praying, fasting and seeking the face of God, the only thing that keeps me giving, keeps me doing what God has called me to do, is the promise I have. I know God is a promise keeper. No matter what my situation looks like, no matter what my circumstances dictate, I know God's Word has gone forth and will not return empty. It must accomplish that unto which it is sent. (Isaiah55:11)

Rebekah's first promise; Divine blessing.

The word *bless* comes from the Hebrew word *barak*, meaning to endue with power for prosperity, longevity, provision, protection, glory, honor and favor. These words speak of success in everything you put your hand to do. It means to be raised to great honor and to receive promotion. God's determination for you and I is for us to be blessed. No man can curse what God has blessed. Number 23:8

How shall I curse, whom God hath not cursed? or how shall I defy, [whom] the LORD hath not defied?

Your beginning was a blessing. Genesis 1:28,

"God blessed them and said be fruitful and multiply, to subdue the land and have dominion.

And so the beginning of man was a blessing.

My beginning was a blessing; your beginning was a blessing. There is no man, no woman, no demon, principality, witch, wizard, warlock, nor sorcerer that can break or nullify what God has blessed. Many times we walk in the place of defeat because we don't know who we are. See—you've got to get to a point in your life where you realize that the time or the season of barrenness you are in is temporary. In other words, your present situation is not your final destination, because **you are blessed!** This season of barrenness is temporary. You are not going to be broke forever. You are not going to ride the bus forever. You are blessed in God, and no man can curse what God has blessed. It is just a test!

We have the assurance that *"the blessing of the Lord, it maketh rich, and adds no sorrow"* (Proverbs 10:22). God wants you to walk in the assurance that **you are blessed!** This is the reason you cannot put a period on someone's life where God has only put a comma. Why? Because a comma means *to be continued*, and it's not over until God says it's over. How dare you declare closure on my case when God has not finished working *with* me and *in* me!

Rebekah's second promise; Supernatural increase.

They blessed her and said, "Sister, may you become the mother of thousands of ten thousands." This is a promise of **enlargement** in all areas. It is a promise of a new stretching that opens up windows of opportunity to receive the supernatural increase God has for you and for me. God wants to increase you. God wants to enlarge you. God wants to increase your house, your business and your ministry!

Because it is the desire of God to increase you, every now and again God will bring us into the season of **contradiction** so that He will gauge a measure of the motive of our hearts before we come into the place of increase. Why do you want Him to give you money? Why do you want to be a millionaire? Is it because you want to live in Beverly Hills and drive a fancy car or is it because you want to be a blessing to somebody? Is it because you want to be a blessing to the nation? Is it because you have a heart for the homeless or the less fortunate? Why do you want God to increase you, to give you the money and the resources you are asking Him for? Is it for a selfish purpose, or is it to help humanity and the work of God?

Many times we ask God to bless us, but our motive for the blessing is wrong. Sometimes God tests you with a little blessing. Do you know the blessing is a test? In other words, He will give you a measure to see what you will do with it. Can He trust you with ten thousand dollars? When He gives you the money what are you going to do with it?

So when God gives you the blessing He watches you and examines your heart. If the first thing you do when you get the money is run to the mall, you just failed the test! If the first thing you do when you get the money is buy yourself a new car when the car you have is still in good working condition, you just failed the test!

I believe God wants to enlarge every area of our lives. I see the capacity the ability to accommodate more of God. There could be more of God in you than you have ever carried before. I see a maturing, a growing up, because God is developing us and enlarging us, increasing us and preparing us to accommodate more of Him and more of His Word. The Lord will enlarge your habitation, your vision. your steps, your heart and your borders. He will enlarge your confession, your chambers and your ministry. That is the second promise given to Rebekah.

Rebekah's third promise; *Victory in warfare.*

God wants you to know you will have victory in your warfare. Please understand child of God that the moment you enlist in this army **get ready for war!**

Many times church folks think coming to church is just peaches and cream, and everything is wonderful. You come and clap your hands, shout unto the Lord, and have a wonderful time. The moment you come into the kingdom of God, **it is warfare!** It was okay as long as your vision was still in the creative process. It was okay as long as your vision was still in your mind and not downloaded out of your mind and into the place called *reality!* But the moment you download the vision from your mind, which is the place of creation, into reality, all hell will break loose!

The whole purpose of the enemy is to abort the vision and miscarry your purpose. You cannot afford to take your warfare lightly. The devil does not sleep, so how is it the children of God are able to sleep until nine in the morning and not even hear the alarm clock? Because they are so tired and are not in their place. They are not watching at their post, praying and waging war with demonic and satanic forces.

The Bible says He gave the promise and the assurance to Rebekah that she would have *victory in warfare* and her descendants would possess the gates of the enemy. To possess the **gates** of the enemy was to occupy the place of authority, power and ultimate control. Biblically **gates** represented the entry point of a city or a town, leading to life or destruction. The word *gate* then became a synonym of power because of the strength and the importance of the gate of the city. Psalm 24:7 the psalmist said:

*"Lift up your heads, O ye **gates**; and be ye lift up, ye everlasting doors; and the King of glory shall come in. Who is the King of glory? The Lord God Almighty."*

In other words, God is saying in whatever capacity, before you can become an overcomer, you must overcome the **gates** of a particular place or city. When I talk about *city,* I am not talking about a geographical location. You can have a **gate** on the city of your heart and that **gate** on your heart resists you. Why? Because you don't have the spiritual tenacity and the resilience in the realm of the Spirit to bring down the **gates** of the enemy through spiritual warfare.

Samson was a very powerful man. He was anointed. The Bible says Samson was so strong that he carried the **gates** of the city. When he went to fight the **gates** of a city—that is, authority, power and ultimate control—he literally lifted up the **gates** of the city, and that was a sign of victory and triumph. Once the **gate** is removed, then the city is vulnerable to the attack. But even though Samson was lifting up **gates** of cities, he was unable to lift up the **gate** of his own heart. So it is not just a question of doing warfare and removing **gates** out of cities and regions and territories. What about the **gates** in your heart that are allowing the spirit of Delilah and the spirits of prostitution and Jezebel to infiltrate your body? You've got to wage war against the **gates** of your heart!

79

They told Rebekah that her seed would possess the **gates** of her enemies. The seeds of Rebekah were Esau and Jacob. Jacob became Israel, and out of Israel came the twelve tribes. Up to today the twelve tribes, when you go to the hundredfold, have possessed the **gates** of their enemies.

In Matthew 16:18 Jesus made the proclamation:

*"I will build my church and the **gates** of hell shall not prevail against it."*

So God is saying He has given us a promise of victory in warfare because He has empowered us to possess the **gates**. **Gates** also represented those who have covenants and administer justice.

Proverbs 8:34:

*"Blessed is the man that heareth me, watching daily at my **gates**, waiting at the posts of my doors."*

If you are an intercessor, you are a watchman at the gate: a gate-keeper. In other words, your responsibility is to guard the gates— the gates of the kingdom, the gates of the church, the gates of the ministry and the gates of the city. When you are a watchman you are guarding the gates because, while activity is going on, a lot of evil stuff will slip in. I'm not talking about a watchman that falls asleep at his post rather being awake at your post. When I talk about being awake, I mean being awake spiritually. You are spiritually awake if you are spiritually vigilant, spiritually alert. You are able to pick up the frequency and to smell stuff before it gets in.

When the children of Israel were delivered out of bondage and captivity with the strong hand of God, through the instrumentality of Moses, the Bible says, over three thousand crossed the Red Sea with Moses. When you continue to read, after they had crossed, the Bible speaks of a company in their midst called *the **mixed multitude***. Exodus 12:38:

And a **mixed multitude** *went up also with them; and flocks, and herds, [even] very much cattle.*

The mixed multitude mingled among the children of God. They just happened to slip in while the Exodus was taking place. They were not Israelites; they were Egyptians. The Israelites had stayed in Egypt for so long, and because there were so many in number it was not easy to discern the Egyptians in their midst until they began to stir up trouble. I can break it down to the hundredfold revelation: even when you come into the kingdom, after God has delivered you out of darkness into the marvelous light, even though you come into the church, you have a tendency to bring some Egypt with you! When you bring Egypt in with you, you still have in you the mixed multitude, with their tendencies and their mixed concepts. Therefore, you find that you have difficulty conforming to this new way of living. Even though you came out of Egypt, there is still a bit of Egypt in you, which is a type of the world.

Egypt was the most powerful kingdom in that time. Egypt was prideful because of who they were and the power they commanded. They literally commanded the entire world. When the move took place with the Israelites; the mixed multitude came in.

They had been with the Israelites for so long that it was almost impossible to tell just by looking whether they were Egyptian or Israelites.

You can be among people that clap like you, sing like you and shout like you, and they know all the "motions" of the church; but they are not like you. That's the reason why according to Judges 12:5,6:

5And the Gileadites took the passages of Jordan before the Ephraimites: and it was [so], that when those Ephraimites which were escaped said, Let me go over; that the men of Gilead said unto him, [Art] thou an Ephraimite? If he said, Nay;

6 Then said they unto him, Say now Shibboleth: and he said Sibboleth: for he could not frame to pronounce [it] right. Then they took him, and slew him at the passages of

Jordan: and there fell at that time of the Ephraimites forty and two thousand.

Before a man could come into a certain territory he had to stand at the gate, open his mouth and say a word. If he was of them, there was a certain way the word was pronounced; then they could identify him. If he was not of them his speech would betray him. If he didn't say it right, it meant he was an imposter!

So how do you begin to identify the mixed multitude? By their manifestation! When you see the different spirits beginning to manifest! Spirits of competition and vainglory. That was not the spirit of Israel. It was the spirit of Egypt (the world). This was the reason, even while they were in the wilderness, God killed the mixed multitude rather than allow them to enter into Canaan lest they polluted the new generation who were born in the wilderness and knew nothing about Egypt. There is nothing new under the sun, according to Solomon. It would be a travesty of justice for you to think God is going to operate with you differently from when He operated with His people back then!

I'm still talking about the gates of the city, that is why the watchman has got to be **alert at the gate!** If he is not alert, he will allow stuff to creep in. Galatians 5:9 says, "*A little leaven leaveneth the whole lump.*" It is the little foxes that destroy the vineyard. But if you are at your watch as the watchman and you are alert and vigilant, you will be able to protect the gate. The Bible says, "Blessed is the man that watches daily at the gate." In other words, he is not going to allow the enemy to go past the gate. He will deal with it at the gate! You have to be alert and aware! Don't take anything for granted! Speech betrays! No one can convince me your words are separated from your heart. The Bible says from the abundance of your heart your mouth will speak. No one knows what is in your heart until you open your mouth. So it is important that gates are watched on a daily basis.

"Blessed is the man who listens to me, watching daily at my gates, waiting at the posts of my doors" (Proverbs 8:34).

The elders and the spiritual authority of God's people sat at the gates. These two Scripture passages speak about gatekeepers.

Deuteronomy 21:19,

"Then shall his father and his mother lay hold on him, and bring him out unto the elders of his city, and unto the gate of his place." Ruth 4:10-11

*10 "Moreover Ruth the Moabitess, the wife of Mahlon, have I purchased to be my wife, to raise up the name of the dead upon his inheritance, that the name of the dead be not cut off from among his brethren, and from the gate of his place: ye are witnesses this day. 11 And all the people that were in the **gate**, and the **elders**, said, we are witnesses. The Lord make the woman that is come into thine house like Rachel and like Leah, which two did build the house of Israel: and do thou worthily in Ephratah, and be famous in Bethlehem."*

God has promised us He will build His church and the gates of hell shall not prevail. All the authority and all the power and evil influence of hell **will not** and **cannot** resist a restored church. It is not easy to infiltrate a church saturated with prayer where people are praying at all watches. When you understand the dimensions, the latitudes and the intensities of prayer, you will realize prayer is a place whereby you have tapped into the realm of God and you know how to access God. Prayer has a language; it has a vocabulary. Prayer has realms and dimensions whereby you are able to go before God and tap into His specific realm. I am not talking about vain repetition rather, being a *sniper* in the realm of the Spirit, because I don't have time to snipe twice! We must know the language and vocabulary! We've got to know our target! We've got to know our position! We've got to be able to measure correctly, before we open our mouths, to be an *effective sniper* in the realm of the Spirit! (Refer to my book Prayer, The Master Key, Raising Prophetic Intercessors In Times Like These)

What do you do when your circumstances are contrary to the promises of God? Often we stay in our circumstances because we have not tapped into that realm of God *called intercessory prayer.* Now hear this, and hear it well! Even when you are tapped into the realm of intercession, nobody tells God *when.* Do you have the nerve to tell God, if He doesn't show up by the end of the week, you are quitting? Guess what God will do? He will let you quit and then let you see what happens to you, because God is God all by Himself! Timing belongs to God. Even though God dwells outside of time, He commands His affairs according to His own time. Four thousand years passed before God sent a Redeemer. Now somebody would have sat down with God and said, "God, if You really loved those people, You should have sent a Redeemer two days later, however even though sometimes it seem like He will not come when you want Him He will always be on time.

God operates in cycles. If God has not finished doing what He wants to do in you, you will not walk in the fulfillment and the manifestation. In every test we go through God is working something in us. A lot of people have preached about Job from the standpoint that He was a righteous man. But when you read deeper you begin to understand the hundredfold dimension that God just didn't want to show Job he was a *righteous* man, but that he was a *self-righteous* man! God was after something deeper. He wasn't just after Job the righteous man, perfect, upright, eschewing evil and fearing the Lord. There was another issue with Job that was hidden out of human sight. God was after the spirit of self-righteousness. For a long time Job was arguing with God based on his self-righteousness. (Job 29). When God was finished trying Job, He turned his captivity and gave him double for the trouble! (Job 42)

All the authority, power and evil influence of hell **will not** and **cannot** resist a restored church. All hell can break loose to frustrate, torment and harass the church, but the devil cannot prevail. Instead the church will batter and break down the gates of hell and set the captives free!

Rebekah received the promise before the fulfillment. Even while she was barren, her future was described as blessed beyond her imagination. She would break out of her barren situation and condition and experience divine blessing, supernatural increase and victory over her enemies. How then did Rebekah respond after hearing all that and yet her circumstances contradicted the promise? **How do you respond to your circumstances when they are contradictory to the promises of God?**

Intercessory Prayer

Key (1) *intercessory prayer*

Genesis 25:21

"And Isaac intreated the Lord for his wife, because she was barren: and the Lord was intreated of him, and Rebekah his wife conceived."

Isaac pleaded with the Lord for his wife. One of the keys to breaking the bands of barrenness is Isaac's response. He pleaded with the Lord. The verb *pleaded*, which comes from the Hebrew *athar*, in this verse is one of the Hebrew words used for intercession. (You can read about the role of a pleader in my book *Prayer, the Master Key)*. It was Isaac's response to stand in the gap for his wife, Rebekah that broke the bonds of wickedness.

One of the key roles of an intercessor is the one of a pleader. The Bible tells us to "come and let us reason together." Isaiah 43:26,

"Put me in remembrance: let us plead together: declare thou, that thou mayest be justified."

In other words, the Word of God is telling us that as a pleader we are similar to an advocate, a pleader in the realm of the Spirit. The word plead is a legal term rendered for one who stands before the judge as a mediator and pleads or defends the case of a client. When you stand as a pleader, you are standing in the gap and pleading on behalf of your client. Whether you are pleading on behalf of your son, daughter, wife or husband. Whether you are pleading on behalf of your nation, city or your church. A pleader must have the language of a pleader. That's the reason that when you go to court you have a lawyer standing on your behalf, going back and forth with the jury and the judge, defending your position according to the legal language and articles. Therefore, as a pleader you've got to know the Word.

When you go before God and you begin to plead you've got to know the verbiage! You've got to know the vocabulary! You've got to be a negotiator in the realm of the Spirit when you go before God. David said, "I have sinned, God, but according to Your loving kindness and Your tender mercies, I come before You. The reason I am pleading with You, God, is because I know You are merciful and long-suffering, and I know You are slow to anger and quick to forgive. So, based on what Your Word says, I am coming before You, asking for clemency." (Psalm51)

The Bible says Isaac entreated the Lord. It was Isaac's response to stand in the gap for his wife, Rebekah, which broke the bands of barrenness. As pleaders, we are provoked by God, and He is challenging us to go before Him in intercession and prayer. In Jeremiah 32:27 God says He is "the God of all flesh." Is there anything too hard for Him? There is nothing impossible unto them that believe. Many times we don't see the breakthroughs we are looking for because we give up too soon. You pray one day, and it doesn't happen! You pray two days, and it doesn't happen! A pleader is similar to an advocate. Intercessory prayer is intensified praying which involves three special ingredients:

- **Identification**: You the intercessor should be able to indentify with the one who is being interceded for. If you don't have a heart for *the person* you are interceding for, your intercession is in vain.
- **Feel the Burden**: The need to *feel the burden*, the pain, the suffering and the needs of the individual. If you have no feelings for the one you're praying for, then you are just wasting time. You should go home and go to bed, because one of the things that motivates prayer and causes the heart of God to move and respond to your prayer and intercession is that you identify with the pain of the person you're interceding for.

You've got to be touched by the feelings of their infirmity. Hebrews 4:15,

"For we have not an high priest which cannot be touched with the feeling of our infirmities." You cannot intercede for me effectively if you don't know how I feel.

- **Go with Authority**: as an intercessor and a pleader, you've got to go with authority. *Exousia* is authority. It simply means the right to exercise without being prohibited, which is the gained position of the intercessor to speak with authority that brings forth results. Isaac positioned himself in intercessory prayer for his barren wife, according to Ezekiel 22:30: *"And I sought for a man among them, that should make up the hedge, and stand in the gap before me."*

Please understand. When you see there is a barren situation in your life, your home, your finances, your church, your region and with a church member, you have the right by the Word, the power of the Holy Spirit and in the name of Jesus, to go before God in intercession. It is not just the Pastors, leaders, or elders that have to pray, we all carry the responsibility to pray.

Deuteronomy 32:30:

"One can put a thousand to flight. Two can put ten thousand."

Isaac prayed for his wife before the bands of barrenness were broken, and there are some bands of barrenness and infertility that will not break until we get into intercession and prayer.

Prayer is the master key. I don't care how much Scripture you know, how many songs you sing, how much praise and worship you have, if you don't know how to access God through prayer, you will not walk in the victory, the power and the manifestation of what God has for you.

Key (2) **A Seeking Heart**

Key number two to intercession is **a seeking heart**. You cannot be an effective intercessor if you don't have a seeking heart. God wants to bring you into a place of fruitfulness, but you have to get into a place of prayer. Some of you are experiencing barrenness, famine and a season of lack, but God is saying you have to get the key, and the key is intercession.

Some of you experience challenges even among your children. If the grades of your children are going down, shouting at your children won't fix them. You have to recognize it, call it what it is and then take it to the next level, knowing this thing is spiritual. Whatever it is that is trying to infiltrate a son or a daughter and bring them into a place of failure, we have the right as parents to take authority in the realm of the Spirit to bind, arrest and neutralize the spirit of ignorance, laziness and lethargy and begin to deposit and decree the spirit of excellence, retention of memory and other positive things. Don't just sit down and talk about it or shout about it, but **pray**. And after you've prayed and interceded, get them some help.

I went through a season when my son transitioned from middle school into high school. Entering a whole new realm, I knew he would have difficulty making the transition. The trouble began with his algebra. I kept getting communication from school that he needed to work harder and push harder and move it up. So I kept telling him and telling him, and then I realized this was spiritual warfare.

I began to write down the different spirits that would try to infiltrate. I recognized that the major spirit was the spirit of distraction. So I began to take authority in the realm of the spirit, and I bound and choked and rendered it neutralized and nullified, disallowed and dismantled the spirit of distraction. Then I began to speak the spirit of focus into his life and the ability to retain what he was taught. I know he has the brain of a genius, but he was being distracted.

After I prayed I took it to the next level and recognized he needed a little extra help. So what did I do? I picked up the phone and called his brother, who is a mathematician, to help him make the transition successfully. So his brother began to come every night and just sit with him for thirty minutes and take him through the dynamics of this thing called mathematics.

It is spiritual warfare, not just a matter of shouting and yelling. You've got to recognize the enemy. You cannot fight the devil until you know the kind of demon you're fighting. And my son got the help, plus prayer and intercession.

Every morning before he went to school I would lay hands on him. I would decree and declare in the name of Jesus that he has the mind of a genius, the mind of a scholar. I had to do all of this in order to help with his transition through that particular season. As a result, he was able to make it.

So what am I saying? It is warfare. When you say there is barrenness somewhere, you've got to go into intercession. It's not just going to happen. If you just sit back and feel wonderful, knowing the Lord is going to do it, it doesn't work that way. You've got to intercede.

Job 5:8,9:

8 "But as for me, I would seek God, and to God I would commit my cause, 9Who does great things, and unsearchable, marvelous things without number."

In seasons of barrenness seek the Lord. The two main Hebrew words for seeking the Lord are *darash* and *baqash*. **Darash** means to tread or frequent, to follow hard after as a pursuer for pursuit or search, to seek, to ask, to make diligent inquiry, to desire something deeply. **Baqash** means to seek to find, to seek to secure, to seek the face of, to desire, to require or to request.

Mark 11:24:

"Therefore I say to you, whatever things you ask when you pray, believe that you receive them, and you will have them."

Intercessory prayer that breaks the bands of barrenness begins with a seeking heart. Read these verses:

Deuteronomy 4:29: *"But from there you will seek the Lord your God, and you will find Him if you seek Him with all your heart and with all your soul."*

1 Chronicles 16:10-11: [10]*"Glory in His holy name; let the hearts of those rejoice who seek the Lord!* [11]*Seek the Lord and His strength; seek His face evermore!"*

1 Chronicles 22:19: *"Now set your heart and your soul to seek the Lord your God. Therefore arise and build the sanctuary of the Lord God, to bring the ark of the covenant of the Lord and the holy articles of God into the house that is to be built for the name of the Lord."*

2 Chronicles 11:16: *"And after the Levites left, those from all the tribes of Israel, such as set their heart to seek the Lord God of Israel, came to Jerusalem to sacrifice to the Lord God of their fathers."*

Job 5:8: *"But as for me, I would seek God, and to God I would commit my cause."*

Psalm 27:8: *"When You said, 'Seek My face,' my heart said to You, 'Your face, Lord, I will seek.'"*

Daniel 9:3: *"Then I set my face toward the Lord God to make request by prayer and supplications, with fasting, sackcloth, and ashes."*

Rebekah had a promise to be fruitful and a promise to be victorious in warfare, but her circumstances contradicted the promises. Isaac did two things to break the bands of barrenness from the life of Rebekah before Rebekah was able to take seed and birth transformation. God is breaking the bands of barrenness in His church and in our lives as individuals. God wants us to be fruitful and multiply. He will increase and enlarge our territory, but before that can happen we've got to do it God's way.

I don't have any gimmicks for you. Everything must be done according to the promise of the Word of God; otherwise it's illegal. The examples we have are in the Word of God. God has given us the assurance that, if it worked for them back then it will work for us today.

As long as you believe, you will receive. That's what the Word of God says in Mark 11:24. Anything that you desire, if you believe, you will receive, but that which initiates the hand of God to move is our desire. What is it you desire to see God do in your life as an individual? What is it you desire to see God do in your family?

Desire is the driving factor that can drive you both negatively and positively. Desire is a force that, if used positively, will bring you the desired results. God is saying Isaac responded the right way when his circumstances were contrary to the promise of God.

Likewise if you do what Issac did, your will get Isaac☐s results and the bands of barrenness will be broken and you will birth the promises of God.

Part 5

Rachel—The Jealousy and Envy Test

※

¹Sing, O barren, thou that didst not bear; break forth into singing, and cry aloud, thou that didst not travail with child: for more are the children of the desolate than the children of the married wife, saith the Lord. ²Enlarge the place of thy tent, and let them stretch forth the curtains of thine habitations: spare not, lengthen thy cords, and strengthen thy stakes; ³for thou shalt break forth on the right hand and on the left; and thy seed shall inherit the Gentiles, and make the desolate cities to be inhabited.—Isaiah 54:1-3

Let's take a closer look at the life of Rachel, the wife of Jacob. Sing, O barren! God is growing in you the fruit of humility and patience. This particular song has more than one stanza. It will require some time for you and me to get in tune. Rachel would later become the mother of Joseph, one of the greatest Old Testament types of Jesus. Rachel is an example to you and me of **endurance in the face of adversity and the birthing of patience and humility.**
Patience means endurance in the face of adversity.

Genesis 29:31:

"And when the Lord saw that Leah was hated, he opened her womb: but Rachel was barren." Then in verse 17 it really

focuses where it states, "Leah was tender eyed; but Rachel was beautiful and well favoured."

One Bible translation says Leah was cross-eyed, but Rachel was beautiful. So keep this in mind as we go on into this lesson.

Many times people have a tendency to believe that based on their outward appearance, their beauty, their gifts, their qualities and their academic excellence it is automatic for them to have what they think they are supposed to have. But it doesn't always work out like that.

Genesis 30:1:

*"And when Rachel saw that she bore Jacob no children, Rachel **envied** her sister; and said unto Jacob, 'Give me children, or else I die.'"*

In that same chapter we read in verses 7 and 8:

7"And Bilhah Rachel's maid conceived again, and bore Jacob a second son. 8And Rachel said, 'With great wrestlings have I wrestled with my sister, and indeed I have prevailed': so she called his name Naphtali."

Here again we see the spirit of compromise where God has not given you what you are seeking at a particular point in time, so you try to help God.

When we do a deep study on this particular lesson concerning patriarchs of old, we begin to see a pattern that is running through the bloodline. The same thing that happened to Abraham happened to Isaac, his son. The same thing that happened to Isaac, happened to Jacob, the son of Isaac. So we must understand that when we are growing in God one of the things we need to look into and reckon with and break is this thing called **generational curses**.

We have raised up a generation of people who are superficial and live in the place called denial. We want to live in a place whereby we would like to believe there is no such thing, but the Bible is clear from Genesis to Revelation where we see numerous accounts of things that happened in the midst of families and in bloodlines that are carried on from one generation to another.

No matter what the environment is geographically or what influence is in that location, there are certain things that would never affect you because it is not a part of your bloodline. Many people want to use that as an excuse all the time, saying it is a result of the generation and the culture in which we live. No, Jesus said that though *we are in the world we are not of the world.* Jesus was able to walk in this earth and not allow anything in the earth realm to affect Him because He knew who He was. Certain things were not a part of His system, (John 14:30) but on the other hand, some things are part of the bloodline. They have been carried down from generation to generation.

Exodus 20:5:

*Thou shalt not bow down thyself to them, nor serve them: for I the LORD thy God [am] a jealous God, visiting the iniquity of the fathers upon the children unto the **third** and **fourth** [**generation**] of them that hate me;*

When we go further in this study we will see in Genesis chapter 31 that one of the issues Rachel had was that she refused to detach herself from the gods of her father. She had an issue with separating herself from the gods of Laban. That is why, after Jacob took his family and left the property of Laban to go and start his own life with his family, Laban pursued Jacob; he wanted his gods back. One day he went to his cupboard where he kept his little idol gods and realized the gods were gone. Guess who had the gods? Rachel. (Genesis 31:34)

When you refuse to detach yourself from certain things that are a part of your family lineage, it is sin. If a man be in Christ, he is a new creature. Behold, all things are passed away, and all things are become new. The moment I became a child of God, the moment I became a new creation, I put every ungodly affiliation away.

That is the reason God began to speak to Abraham. He told him, "Come out from among your people. Separate yourself. Come out from the familiar and go to the place that I will show you." But Abraham did not obey God completely. He started to go, but he made a stop in another place. God said, "That's not where I told you to stop."(paraphrase). But Abraham was still battling with the gods of his father until Terah died.

There are things in our lives that have to die before we can move on to do what God has called us to do. There are some habits, behaviors, beliefs and some cultures that have come down your bloodline generationally and have become an accepted norm. When you say that's the way the family has always been and nobody can do anything about it, the devil is a liar. We are struggling with generational issues, and people seek counseling and help, but the whole point is that they are refusing to identify or acknowledge the spirit that has giving the enemy legal access into their lives.

What has given that spirit jurisdictional rights to come into your territory? Unless you have something that belongs to that spirit it will not invade you. Mice don't go to a place where there is no cheese. Rachel had her father's gods, and when Laban began to pursue them, Jacob was confused. He asked, "Why are you pursuing us? I've done everything that is right in your sight. I've given you what belongs to you. I don't have anything that belongs to you that gives you jurisdictional rights to pursue me."

But what Jacob did not know was that Rachel, his wife, had something underneath her skirts that belonged to Laban (a type of the devil), and the devil will not let you go until you release what belongs to him. Stuff doesn't just happen. People live in denial. If you don't know where the spirit came from, then it behooves you to go back and do research on your family lineage to find out what happened years ago to your father, your grandfather and great-grandfather. If you don't, generations later something will show up in your seed and your seeds seed. What you condone, will control you. What you don't confront, will eventually confine you and hinder you from your blessing.

We see a pattern, and it is serious because it's a blood thing. It runs in the blood. It takes the blood of Jesus to break that blood pattern. It is not something you can just lay hands on and it's gone. Oh, no, it's not going. It requires you to dig deep with the mantle and with the anointing of Jeremiah, which is to root out, pull down and destroy then build and plant. (Jeremiah 1:10)

Parents, when you begin to see character traits manifesting in your child, do not take it lightly. Some people will say he's just being a child. No, he's not just being a child. That is the beginning, that is the sign and the symptom, and you have to nip it in the bud before it becomes a tree. If you don't bend it while it is yet tender, then you have no choice but to break it.

So before we can birth patience and humility we must pass the jealousy and envy test.

2 Corinthians 10:12:

"For we dare not make ourselves of the number, or compare ourselves with some that commend themselves: but they measuring themselves by themselves, and comparing themselves among themselves, are not wise."

The Bible says that when Rachel saw she bore no children for Jacob, Rachel was envious of her sister, Leah. Many of us are experiencing barrenness because of the spirit of **jealousy and envy**. If you are going to fulfill the purpose of God in your life, there comes a time when we need to confront our own demons. You cannot cover up all the time. As church folks, we know how to dress it up, how to make it look good, how to match it and accessorize; but you don't want to deal with what's underneath. We are used to covering up, and God says until we get to the place where we lay bare and confront our own demons we are not going to be able to come into the arena of deliverance.

Jealousy is not an easy emotion or mindset to admit or keep under wraps once it starts, but one conclusion is certain. Everyone deals with this subtle enemy in life, in church and in the ministry at some point in their life. Jealousy comes with varying degrees of potency. A little spot of jealousy seems easily conquerable when need be, but it comes and goes and seldom lingers; but before you realize it, jealousy is in full manifestation. People have a tendency to say, "I'm not jealous about anybody. I've got everything I need." But that is not always true.

Jealousy does not just manifest outwardly. Jealousy manifests through your words. The condition of our heart is known by the words that come out of your mouth. Somebody may look at you and think you are not bothered at all, but the moment you open your mouth your words will betray you.

It may be an illogical prejudgment of another person, such as, "He doesn't deserve it," or "I can't believe he got that," or "It's not fair." In other words, what you're saying is,

"It should have been me. I do all the hard work"; or "He's probably compromising something else in order to have that."

Jealousy may manifest over someone's beautiful home or jewelry, someone's skin color, figure, hair or intelligence, their marriage, even their ministry or business. You will see a hint of jealousy when someone pulls up in a brand-new Mercedes and calls everyone over to celebrate with him, and then you make a comment such as, "I liked the other car," or "I really prefer the other one."

The reason you would make such a comment is that you actually wish you could have the new car yourself, but because you are not in a position to have it and because of the bitterness and resentment in your spirit you make a nasty comment that is out of the spirit of jealousy. It manifests itself in so many different ways. Someone who is in the spirit of jealousy is always critical about other people because they desire what the other person has. You might make a comment like, "It would have been better if she had worn her hair this other way." The reason you would make that comment is that you really do like the way her hair is, but you don't have the ability to get yours to look like that.

And jealousy may manifest over someone's marriage. You know the couple is happily married, but you always have a negative comment to make because you haven't got a husband or a wife yet. So every now and again you release a comment that you are perfectly satisfied being single, because you can go, do whatever you want when you want. The reason you say this is that you are jealous of the person who is already married and that's what you really want. We must kill the spirit of jealousy because jealousy is cruel, destructive and swift. Its invigorating flame consumes character and destroys beauty.

Song of Solomon 8:6b:

> ... *jealousy [is] cruel as the grave: the coals thereof are coals of fire, [which hath a] most vehement flame.*

What is envy? Envy is a feeling of uneasiness around the person that is envied. This harbored feeling of envy is aroused when surveying the excellence prosperity or happiness of another. You get a bad feeling when you are around someone you envy. Every time you see that person, you get a bad taste in your mouth and you break out in a sweat. Why? Because you secretly desire to be in that person's position, but you cannot be in that position; so every time he or she is around you, instead of celebrating them, you get a bad taste in your mouth.

God is about to give you a breakthrough. You may say with your mouth that you are not jealous, but what does your body say? Why does your heart start beating faster every time that person comes in? Why does your adrenalin rush? Why do you break out in a sweat? Why do you suddenly see that your countenance has fallen the moment that individual walks in? Even though you don't say anything, your body language is saying you are envious of that person. You know this feeling when you are pained by the desire of possessing some superior thing that another possesses.

With envy come other emotions—rivalry, comparison, malice, grudging and criticism. When you know you are lacking in a certain area and then see a sister who has what you really want, that's when you begin to compare yourself. The Bible says he who compares himself with others is not wise. Maybe God blessed your sister a little more in one area, and you don't have that kind of blessing, so when your sister comes up, instead of complimenting the blessing, you criticize the blessing. The only reason you are being critical is because you wish you had more of what she has.

God created each and every one of us different, and some of us just have a little more grace than others in certain areas. This is the reason the plastic surgery industry is prospering, because everything is rooted out of jealousy. People are ready to spend thousands of dollars because they want to look like someone else. So when you hear people making comments that are rooted in the spirit of jealousy, it is because of the blessing they don't have but wish they had.

I'm talking about jealousy and envy, the spirit of Rachel. When you have that spirit, nothing anyone else does is good enough. There is always something wrong with what everyone else does. It always has to be your chicken that tastes the best. No one else's chicken can be compared to your chicken because yours always has to be the best. This is rooted out of the spirit of jealousy and envy. When the table is laid out, you look to see which dish most people are going to. So when the spirit of jealousy and envy is in you, something rises up, and before you realize it you find a way to go behind the table, withdraw that dish and put yours there.

Envy has been the demise of many great leaders and the pollution of pure wells. We must identify what it really is. We cover it with a lot of things. We call it a lot of things, but the real thing is just the spirit of jealousy and the spirit of envy. When someone does something you don't appreciate, you criticize it; that is nothing but the spirit of jealousy and envy. Envy, which is the pain, the uneasiness or discontentment ignited by the sight of another's superiority or success, is always accompanied by some degree of hatred or malignancy, and often a desire or an effort to depreciate the other person or to take pleasure in seeing that person's depreciation. Envy springs from pride, ambition and jealousy.

In Scripture, envy and jealousy are usually accompanied by murder, strife, deceit, malice and other issues that bring rottenness to the soul.

Job 5:2, "For *wrath killeth the foolish man, and envy slayeth the silly one.*"

Proverbs 14:36 says, "*A sound heart is the life of the flesh: but envy the rottenness of the bones.*"

Proverbs 27:4 says, "*Wrath is cruel, and anger is outrageous; but who is able to stand before envy?*"

Jealousy and envy will make you barren and unfruitful. Genesis 30:1 says that when Rachel saw she bore Jacob no children she *envied* her sister and said to Jacob, "Give me children, or I die."

The words *jealous* and *envious* are interchangeable. They both stem from an unhealthy need to compare. Rachel was in the barren category, and Leah was in the blessed and productive category, the category that was without effort. She was just producing effortlessly. Rachel was in the category of barrenness, infertility and sterility and found herself thinking, "If only I could be successful in the same way, then I would be fulfilled." **This is the tragedy of the spirit of jealousy and envy.**

When you see someone who is successful and prospering, when you see someone's marriage blossoming, the spirit of jealousy and envy rises up because you are in a season of barrenness and infertility. Then the enemy deceives you into believing that if only you could be like that person you would be fulfilled. People try to define who they are supposed to be by comparing themselves with other people. Therefore, it is unwise for you to compare yourself with anyone else.

You are who you are, and I am who I am. God will raise me up; God will raise you up. God will use me; God will use you. God will promote us based on our uniqueness and our peculiar qualities. I do not need to be like you for God to bless me.

A lot of times we are in trouble because we are trying to become a cheap copy instead of being an original. God has created you to be an original. You are peculiar; and different; You are fearfully and wonderfully made (Psalm 139:14). That's what makes you unique and spectacular. That's what makes me who I am, and you who you are. God is not in the business of manufacturing clones.

I cannot measure my success by comparing myself to you. That is the way God chose to make you successful, and I bless and celebrate you; but I know also that God has something unique for me. So I'm going to wait until God brings me into my season of fruitfulness, abundance and blessing.

Rachel found herself thinking, "If only I could be successful, if only I could produce like Leah, I would then be fulfilled." Before Rachel could birth Joseph, who signifies **patience and humility**, her heart's motive had to be right.

The Right Motive

God is not so much concerned about what you do as He is about why you do it. What is the real reason? Why do you need God to turn your barrenness into fruitfulness? What's the reason behind what you are doing? What's the real reason behind why you pray? Are you praying because you love God? Or are you praying because you are trying to manipulate God?

That's what Rachel was doing. She tried to manipulate Jacob, as many of us try to manipulate God. She said, *"Give me children, or I die"* (Genesis 30:1).

But God says, "Who cares if you die? I'm still God. If you think you are going to get what you want the way you want it, I'm going to show you I am still God, and I cannot be manipulated or intimidated."

What is the real reason you need God to turn your barrenness into fruitfulness? What's behind the prize? You want children, growth, success and influence. You want power, notoriety, favor and recognition, or else you will die. This is not a physical death, but the death of your vision, your faith, your joy, your passion, your esteem and your honor. In other words, "God, if You don't do it, how will others see me? You've got to do it, God, because I have an image to maintain. I am the Woo-Woo from the land of Too-Too, and I've already established a reputation. So based on my reputation, God, You've got to do something to protect it. So whichever way You do it, just do it."

This insatiable appetite for producing simply to impress people and prove you are somebody is one of the most subtle traps of the enemy in every sphere, whether business, the corporate world, your marriage or even your ministry. The driving force behind what you do is important. What is the driving force behind your desire to have a successful business? Is it because you want to prove to others that you too are making it?

God wants to break the bands of barrenness, but before He can do that we must deal with certain things.

In ministry, success can be spelled in larger attendance, more numbers, better programs, bigger buildings and so on. Therefore, if our motives are wrong and if we are asking for the wrong reason, God will give Leah, your sister ministry; four sons (productivity) before moving on to Rachel to teach, to instill, to develop and then to birth the kingdom principle of **patience and humility**.

God has a way of blessing your next-door neighbor to provoke you to seek Him in the right way and with the right motive. He will bless the person next to you who has fewer qualities and is not as well educated, endowed and talented as you. God will allow that to happen in order to provoke you and to push you to go to Him for the right reason and with the right motive.

Character

Your gifting and potential do not move God. It is your character. **Character is; the inherent complex of attributes that determine a persons moral and ethical actions and reactions; ones behavior defines them as a person of a specified kind (usually with many eccentricities).** In other words your gift (charisma) defines your potential, but your character determines your legacy.

Rachel was the fourth wife of a patriarch to suffer barrenness, but God was making it apparent that human ambition and human services were not responsible for carrying on the promises of God. Rachel was the favored wife of Jacob. Rachel was beautiful physically and in every other way. She had everything outwardly, but she soon found out that unless God intervened, her beauty could not acquire her desires.

You can have all the qualities academically, intellectually and physically, but if your character is out of line, God is not going to comply. God is not impressed with your gifting; God is impressed with your character. Please understand your gift may get you there, but your character will keep you there. A lot of people get into places by their gifts, but the reason they are out in the next two weeks is that their character stinks. If you think because you have a gift it gives you the right to go into a place and behave any kind of way, talk to your leaders any kind of way, behave the way you want, then your character is out of line, and what your gift brought to you, your character will cause you to lose.

Many people today are intellectually sound and academically powerful, and they have everything it takes to become successful, but the reason they are not where they are supposed to be is that their character is out of line. They don't know how to behave; they don't know how to say please, thank you, excuse me or I'm sorry. This is a basic character requirement, but you just don't know how to say you are sorry.

If you are late to your job and your supervisor confronts you, all you have to do is humble yourself and say, "I'm sorry." Don't try to justify yourself. It may get you fired no matter what your credentials are. If you think the company needs you more than you need it, that's a lie. It's a mutual thing. They need you, and you need them. So don't go in there with an attitude. Just because you are the computer technician and without you everything would come to a standstill when the computer crashes. The devil is a liar.

Seven thousand have not bowed their knee to Baal. Believe me, there are thousands of graduates on the waiting list, so you should count it a privilege you got the job. You should handle the job as if it's gold. If you have an attitude because of your little gift, I reiterate that the devil is a liar.

Outwardly Rachel was beautiful, talented and gifted, but inwardly her character stank. Her jealousy was unacceptable and inexcusable, and her impatient carnality caused harmful results. Let me bring this home. Ladies, your beauty alone is not what will get you a husband. It is not just about lips, hips and fingertips. When you get married and you finally settle down and you take off the eyelashes and the nails, the man is going to be looking for something more than your lips, your hips and your fingertips, and that is called character.

Proverbs 31:30:

Favour is deceitful, and beauty [is] vain: but a woman that feareth the LORD, she shall be praised.

The Bible said Leah was cross-eyed, or tender eyed, and God opened Leah's womb, but Rachel was beautiful and could not produce. If you don't know how to cook, you have no housekeeping skills, and you don't communicate well—learn. Your tongue must be seasoned with salt. The Bible says in Proverbs 31:26, "*Upon her tongue was the law of kindness.*" If you are standing on your beauty, I guarantee you, if you are not careful you'll be kicked out, and in will come Leah. Leah is cross-eyed, but she can cook; Leah is cross-eyed, but she can clean; Leah is cross-eyed, but she knows how to treat a man. Leah is cross-eyed, but she respects her man.

Some of you are lazy. You don't know how to keep your room; you don't know how to put your stuff together, your shoes in the bathroom, dirty dishes in the sink, you are completely disorganized. Just because you're beautiful and you think you're all that and a bag of chips that is not what keeps a man. It takes more than that to keep a man. You come home, and all you do is lounge in the chair. All you know how to do is bring home takeout food every night. You had better take off your eyelashes, take off your nails, remove that wig and get in the kitchen and cook your husband a proper meal. If you think he can't live without you I've got news for you. He *can* live without you. I assure you the strange woman is waiting around the corner.

Proverbs 7:8-10:

8 Passing through the street near her corner; and he went the way to her house, 9 In the twilight, in the evening, in the black and dark night: 10 And, behold, there met him a woman with the attire of an harlot, and subtil of heart.

It is not just about your looks. It takes more than looks. But now let me bring it down to the men. It's not about your car, money or your house. It takes more than that. The woman needs to be loved. She needs affection. She needs you. If you think you're the best hunk in town and you've got plenty of money, I've got news for you. It takes more than just biceps and triceps and good cologne.

A woman's number one requirement is affection. A man's number one requirement is respect. If you give everything in the natural, but if you don't give affection or respect, then you have nothing. Please understand brother, this is why you have difficulty. Women are the easiest creatures to deal with. They are complicated, but they are easy. A woman can be as mad as mad can be, and then you show up with flowers, and suddenly she is just so sweet. I don't want to turn this book into a book on marriage, but I do want to talk to the brothers a little more.

Don't talk *to* her; talk *with* her. There is a difference between talking *to* and talking *with*. When you come home and you're hungry, don't just go to her demanding your dinner and questioning her about what she has done all day. How about asking in a kind way? "What's for dinner tonight, honey?" It makes such a difference. Submission is a learned and love behavior. Domion is a created behavior. When God created them male and female, He gave them dominion. *Them.*

So, therefore, dominion is a created thing, and that's why if you use the wrong tools you get the wrong results. You don't get submission from dominance. You have to use the right tools if you're looking for the right results.

Ephesians 5:25:

"Husbands, love your wives as Christ loved the church,"

When you love her as Christ loved the church, even to the point of giving up your life for her, her submission to you will come easy.

Outwardly Rachel was beautiful, but in her angry jealous state she questioned the wisdom of God and demanded from Jacob what he could not give to break the bands of barrenness. Rachel threatened Jacob with her unreasonable demands. "Give me children lest I die."

Jacob responded in anger and said, *"Am I in the place of God who has withheld from you the fruit of the womb?"* (Genesis 30:2). In other words, he was saying, "I'm not the one responsible for your barrenness. God is. If you are looking for someone to break the bands of barrenness, you'd better go to the One who has the power to break it."

Jacob understood that both fruitfulness and its absence are under the divine will and control of God Himself. Just because you have what it takes does not automatically qualify you. Your attitude determines your altitude. Rachel, stop blaming Jacob. Wife, stop blaming your husband, Husband stop blaming your wife. Saints, stop blaming the pastor, pastor, stop blaming the saints. Businessmen, stop blaming your accountants and your partners. Accountants and partners, stop blaming the businessmen. They are not God.

Only God has the Answer

Jacob's answer to Rachel was the only answer. "I am not standing in the place of God." There is a God in heaven who is sovereign, and His ways and thoughts are higher than ours (Isaiah 55:8-9).

Daniel 2:21:

"And he changeth the times and the seasons: he removeth kings, and setteth up kings: he giveth wisdom unto the wise, and knowledge to them that know understanding."

God does not feel any pressure to hurry His plan and His purpose. He does according to His will and none can stop His hand or question what He is doing.

Jeremiah 18:6:

"Cannot I do with you as this potter? saith the Lord."

In other words, God is the potter, and we are just the clay. Because God is the potter, He has the right to do what He wants, how He wants and when He wants. God is not an indulgent father who gives His children whatever they desire whenever they desire it irrespective of moral and spiritual considerations.

Even we as ministers and teachers are not responsible for the spiritual outcome of our prayers and supplications to God. We are responsible for positioning the church and ministering in the Spirit, in faith, in the heart attitude and with eyes focused on nobody but God. My job is to bring you to a place where you are not looking at the man or the woman, but looking at God. My job and my assignment are to direct you to the true and living God. A man, a woman, will fail you, but God will never fail you. Man is mortal. God is immortal. Man is mutable (capable of or tending to change in form or quality or nature). God is immutable (not subject to change or variation in form, quality or nature). Man is temporary; God is eternal. And so you cannot keep your eyes on a person as opposed to God. That's the reason God says, "I'm not just doing something, but I'm doing a deep work in the midst of My people. And I'm thinking of people even in your life." In other words, a day will come when God will remove me, but if you do not learn to look to God for yourself, what will you do when God moves me out?

It would behoove you to learn how to access God for yourself. My assignment is to teach you how to pray, teach you how to fast, teach you how to study the Word, teach you how to seek God for yourself, teach you how to take hold of the horns of the altar and, finally, teach you how to be delivered.

People come and people go, but God is eternal. If you are drawn by a personality, you will miss your visitation. It is wonderful because God uses people, but people are not God. When Moses went Joshua showed up. The children of Israel had a problem with the changing of the tenure because they were still caught up in Moses. God reassured them in Joshua 1:5 that as He was with Moses, He would be with Joshua.

God will not tolerate idolatry. Never bring a man or a woman of God to a place of an idol because you will cause God to remove them before their time. They are just a vessel, instruments that God is using. You cannot keep your eyes fixed on a personality for your deliverance or for your healing. Their job is to show you where the Deliverer and the Healer is even Jesus Christ the Son of the Living God. Therefore that brings them to a place whereby they are not responsible for the manifestation of the Word of God. God is. All glory, credit and greatness must always be ascribed to Him alone.

We need to learn. Some people will get an attitude and get it twisted because they are locked up in an individual. You must learn to look to God, and God can use any one of you. It doesn't need to be me. God can pick any one of you and raise you up and use you even greater than he has used me, because God is no respecter of persons but is a respecter of principles. (Acts 10:34-35)

Jeremiah 18:6 reads, *"Cannot I do with you as this potter? saith the Lord."* Again, God is not an indulgent father who just gives to you whenever you desire. God is bent on teaching principles that will uphold you for the rest of your life. I am living today on the principles I have learned. If I had not learned to access God for myself, I would not be able to stand today. But I maximized my time with my teachers and my mentors, and I learned everything I could. I learned how to access God for myself. God taught me how to study and how to speak in faith. He taught me how to pray and how to fast. As a result of that now I am able to stand and to represent God.

When you attend church, be serious about God. When the Word is being preached, take it in. Be sure to write notes. A lot of people sit in church thinking they can remember it, but they can't remember anything. So you should take as much as you can while you can.

Jesus told the disciples in John 14:19:

"A little while and ye shall not see me; and again a little while and ye shall see me because I go to the Father."

The disciples were so powerful they literally impacted the world because for the season they were with their teacher they took in everything and learned how to access God for themselves. As a result, when Jesus was taken away they were able to continue the work of the ministry.

Even ministers and leaders should never try to make people think they are God. A leader should never bring people to a place where they think they cannot live without the leader. Everything a leader does should point to Jesus. I'm not the healer, but Jesus is. I'm the mediator between you and Jesus, and so I pray on your behalf to God. I pray in the name of Jesus, Lord, heal Your servant. I believe God will flow through me as an instrument and heal you. But we should never portray ourselves as if we are the healer or the deliverer. God will cut us off before our time.

We are responsible for positioning our churches and our ministries in the Spirit, in faith and with a heart attitude with eyes focused on an awesome God. Leaders position, God provides, and God produces. Patience is a fruit of the Spirit. Gifts are given; fruit is grown. Therefore, it is a process. We are always in a hurry, but God will not be manipulated into premature actions. Nobody can tell God what to do, when to do, how to do. Don't do that. You will be in trouble. Some people have the nerve to give God a deadline. Guess what. God will not show up, but He will see if you are going to quit. He will not be manipulated into premature action.

When He chooses to allow barrenness for a season, He is working according to His perfect plan. When God seems to be slow, it is because He desires for us to recognize His full knowledge and perfect control of every circumstance that arises in our lives. Sometimes we feel as if God has left us. But even though Rachel and Jacob could not see God standing in the shadows, He was there with His unerring hand. Psalm 46:1 says God is "a very present help in time of trouble." Just hold on and let God work. Genesis 30:22 says, *"And God remembered Rachel."* God is about to remember you.

You've been through hell and high water, but God is about to remember you. You've been in the valley, but God is about to remember you. The devil thought it was over, but it is not over until God says it's over. Why? Because your present situation is not your final destination. God is a God of remembrance. He is the same God who remembered Abraham, the same God who remembered David, the same God who remembered Hannah, and the same God who remembered Rachel. Because He is a God of remembrance, He is about to remember you and me.

People may have talked about you, looked at you funny, treated you unjustly, but I've got news for you. It's not going to last forever. God is about to remember you. You've been barren, unfruitful and sterile. Leah has had her children; her prosperity and her abundance. And through it all it looked as if nothing was going to happen for you, but I came to make an announcement. It's your season!.

People may have forgotten about you, people you've helped, prayed and fasted for, people you gave your life for. They will forget about you, but our Father God will never forget for He is a God of remeberance.

Oh, yes, the butler forgot about Joseph even as he was leaving the prison. Joseph said to him, "Please, when you go to Pharaoh, remember me." The Bible says in Genesis 40:23, "When he went out, the butler forgot about him." God was planning to teach him a lesson, that you cannot put your trust in men.

You must be able to put your trust in God, and that is why David said in

Psalm 20:7: "*Some trust in chariots, and some in horses, but we will remember the name of the Lord.*"

Psalm 125:1: "*They that put their trust in God shall be as Mount Zion which cannot be removed but abideth forever.*" The Lord surrounds His people.

David was confused and asked God a question. He said, "Why do the wicked prosper? I'm Your child, and I serve You. I do everything You tell me to do. I walk in obedience and faith.."

And God came to David in Psalm 37:1 and said, "*Fret not.*" He said not to fret because your season is coming; your time is coming. And God remembered Rachel. When the gynecologists of Israel forgot about Sarah, God remembered Sarah. When the butler forgot about Joseph, God remembered Joseph. When God remembers you, guess what. He works quickly.

When you go to Malachi 3:16, you read that the Lord wrote the book of remembrance. There is a book of remembrance, and written in that book is your name, and written in that book are your prayers, your supplications and your intercessions. In that book are written all your petitions, all the tears you have cried, and God is saying to bring the book of remembrance, and He's asking for the track record on each of the brethren. When the book of remembrance was brought, God remembered. God is about to remember you, whether the devil likes it or not.

The Bible says God remembered Rachel and listened to her, and He opened her womb. No more barrenness. The bands of barrenness were broken when the timing of the Lord was perfect. God completed a work in Rachel that no other test could have afforded. In the fullness of time Rachel birthed Joseph, and Rachel praised God.

Part 6

Manoah's Wife

[1] Sing, O barren, thou that didst not bear; break forth into singing, and cry aloud, thou that didst not travail with child: for more are the children of the desolate than the children of the married wife, saith the Lord. [2] Enlarge the place of thy tent, and let them stretch forth the curtains of thine habitations: spare not, lengthen thy cords, and strengthen thy stakes; [3] for thou shalt break forth on the right hand and on the left; and thy seed shall inherit the Gentiles, and make the desolate cities to be inhabited.—Isaiah 54:1-3

Joel 3:10, "*Let the weak say, I am strong.*" I believe God is going to birth strength in His body. A lot of times we get hit by the enemy, and the warfare intensifies. When the warfare intensifies, our defenses are weakened. God wants you to know He is getting ready to birth strength.

In Judges 13:1-2:

[1] "And the children of Israel did evil again in the sight of the Lord; and the Lord delivered them into the hand of the Philistines forty years. [2] And there was a certain man of Zorah, of the family of the Danites, whose name was Manoah; and his wife was barren, and bare not."

Through the womb of Sarah, the wife of Abraham, we saw the birthing of laughter, which was a sign of conquest, through the coming forth of Isaac. We saw through the womb of Rebekah, the birth of transformation and change whereby Jacob became Israel. We saw through the womb of Rachel the birthing of patience and humility with the birth of Joseph, who was symbolic of patience and humility.

Now we are dealing with another barren woman who is not named in the Bible. She is simply mentioned as Manoah's wife. It is significant that this woman is unnamed, because the greatest exploits of God are wrought in prayer by nameless, unsung heroes of the church who are the intercessors. They are people who are nameless and faceless, and yet they are working great exploits in the kingdom of God through the invisible ministry of prayer and intercession. Things are being birthed in the kingdom of God through these nameless and faceless people.

It's not always a case of your name being in the limelight so you would be deemed powerful and effective in the kingdom of God. Some of the most powerful organs of your body are invisible. You cannot see them, but if they stopped working your visible body would literally come to a standstill. Your heart is not visible, but your heart is the most integral organ of your body. Your kidneys are not visible, but they are the filters that cleanse toxins from your blood without which we would be poisoned by our own waste products. Your liver is not visible, but it is our body's primary detoxification organ. Therefore, you cannot despise any member of the body. Every member of the body, both visible and invisible, is important.

And so the Bible does not name this woman. She is simply termed as Manoah's wife. The Bible makes us to understand that according to Judges 13:1-2, God visited this couple and announced the birthing of something that was to be the beginning of the deliverance of the nation of Israel. In this Scripture passage the Israelites had gone into a place of disobedience whereby they had turned to idolatry and away from serving the Lord their God and so God's hand was lifted from them.

Any time you turn away from serving God, God will turn away from you. God will literally shut the heavens on you. God would withdraw His hand of mercy, and this was the situation of the nation of Israel at this particular time.

The Bible leads us to understand that God had delivered the children of Israel into the hands of the Philistines. These were turbulent times in which there was no king in Israel. Every man did that which was right in his own eyes, according to Judges 21:25. When you go back and study, you will find that the Bible says it was a time when everybody was doing what was right in his own eyes, and therefore God shut the heavens. The heavens became like brass. There was no open vision, and literally a famine hit the nation of Israel. The strength of God had departed.

Anytime we turn away from serving God and serve other gods or worship self, our strength diminishes. The strength of the Lord had departed. Therefore, there was no resistance against the Philistines, who were the enemies of God's people. The spirit of the Philistines had provoked all great anointings and great unctions.

It was the Philistines who attacked David, or the kingship anointing. It was the Philistines who attacked Isaac. Remember that Isaac is the compass anointing, who has the power to dig up underground wells and resources, and when any kind of anointing of that magnitude begins to arise, the spirit of the Philistines comes and launches an attack. It was the Philistines who attacked Samson, which was strength.

The spirit of the Philistines is a spirit of disruption, frustration, presumption, seduction, control, oppression and harassment. It's the spirit that defies, ridicules and mocks the people of God. Therefore, we need to put down the spirit of the Philistines, because the Philistines were out to destroy the people of God.

God wants us to sing, O barren, because strength is being birthed. When the spirit of the Philistines attacks, the people of God are weakened. Your prayer life weakens; the study of the Word weakens; your fasting routine weakens. Everything concerning your regimen with God weakens, and that's one of the signs that the Philistines have attacked you.

God wants you to know that when strength is birthed and when strength is released, He gives it to us, the body of Christ, so that we are able to destroy, nullify and neutralize the spirit of the Philistines.

Manoah's wife conceived and gave birth to one who personified strength. Even though we are weak and sometimes feel defeated, God wants us to know that resident within us He is birthing strength.

2 Corinthians 12:9-10:

9 "And he said unto me, My grace is sufficient for thee: for my strength is made perfect in weakness. Most gladly therefore will I rather glory in my infirmities, that the power of Christ may rest upon me. 10Therefore I take pleasure in infirmities, in reproaches, in necessities, in persecutions, in distresses for Christ's sake: for when I am weak, then am I strong."

When the attack is so great and intense, there is a tendency to grow weary and to tire. Anybody would begin to feel tired and weary when you've been on the battlefront and the attack is so intense and you have been hit from every side, on the left and on the right, in your family and among your peers. It seems you are in a constant battle. But when you are weak He is strong. You don't have to depend on your own strength. We are not sufficient of ourselves, but our sufficiency is in the Lord. And God wants you to understand strength will be birthed in Jesus' name.

Individuals are tired; the church is tired; single mothers are tired; the body of Christ is tired. We are going to have to sing and press through till we break through. Don't grow weary. I know it's hard and the battle is intensifying. I know the enemy has turned up the heat, but God is saying to press through until you break through, till souls are birthed into the kingdom.

It is not easy to birth souls into the kingdom. In fact it's not easy to birth anything, no matter what it is. There is going to be a level of travail. There will be a level of warfare and some kind of fight before you birth what God wants you to birth. Thus we need strength. But we don't need just any kind of strength. We need supernatural strength, which is the opposite of weakness. In other words, Manoah's wife overcame her weakness and her barrenness, and before you and I can overcome our weaknesses and our barrenness, we need to understand three principal keys.

(1) **Marry the Right Man**

Key number one is being married to the right man. The only way you and I can overcome our weakness and come into the place where we are able to birth strength is by being married to the right man. Manoah's wife was barren, and she was weak, but she was married to the right man; that was Manoah. In the case of the kingdom and in the body of Christ, you've got to be married to the husband Jesus Christ. There is no way you and I can overcome the attacks of the enemy and the intensity that is coming up against us until we are married to Jesus Christ.

The Bible says we must be born again. In other words, you cannot expect God to work on your behalf when you don't have a committed covenant relationship with God. Many people want what God has, but they don't want a relationship with God. They want His power, His protection, His healing and His deliverance. They want Him to open doors for them, but they don't want to enter into a relationship with Him. So God is saying it's timeout for playing games.

It's timeout for you having one foot in the church and one foot in the world. It's timeout for you thinking you can just grab the healing, the blessing and the anointing and then just walk out. God said it's time for you to make a covenant commitment. You've got to come into a covenant relationship with God. You've got to say yes to His will and yes to His way. You've got to make a commitment as Ruth made a commitment to Naomi and say, *"Your people will be my people. Your God will be my God. Where thou goest I will go"* (Ruth 1:16).

The Bible makes us understand that without Him we are nothing and without Him we can do nothing. He is the true vine, and we are the branches; until we are connected to the vine we have no power, no wisdom, no understanding. We've got to make a commitment. We've got to have that connection. Manoah's wife had that connection. She was married to the right man.

We must be regenerated by being born again. Ephesians 5:22-33 speaks about a marriage. The Word of God is likened unto a marriage. You've got to make a commitment. You must be able to make the vow. When you say that vow you must be able to mean it.

Don't come to God just because you have a need or just because you are sick and need to be healed. Don't come to God just because you are broke, busted and disgusted and then pretend you are for God; then the moment God gives you your miracle, your healing, you don't know who God is and you don't even know where He lives.

Let me tell you, what you thought was your deliverance, what you thought was your healing, if you came with a mindset to pimp God, it's not going to last. Only what you do for Christ will last.

The Bible says she was married to the right man by the name of Manoah and they lived in a place called Zorah. The name *Zorah* means a nest of hornets. Her husband was named Manoah, like Noah, which means rest. In other words, God's rest is enough for your nest. As long as you are married to the right man, you don't have to worry about the hornet's nest.

Ephesians 2:14 says Jesus is our peace. Peace is a realm. Peace is a dimension, and rest is a realm. So the first key God wants you to understand is that, before you can bring forth strength and be delivered from weakness into the place of strength, you've got to be married to the right man.

(2) Set Aside Your Strength
Manoah's wife set her strength aside for the work of the Lord.

Judges 13:3-5:

3 "And the angel of the Lord appeared unto the woman, and said unto her, Behold now, thou art barren, and bearest not: but thou shalt conceive, and bear a son. 4Now therefore beware, I pray thee, and drink not wine nor strong drink, and eat not any unclean thing: 5For, lo, thou shalt conceive, and bear a son; and no razor shall come on his head: for the child shall be a Nazarite unto God from the womb: and he shall begin to deliver Israel out of the hand of the Philistines."

Before God can release you out of weakness and bring you into the strength of God, you've got to set your strength aside for the work of the Lord. When you birth strength, your strength must be

118

sanctified. Your strength must be placed into a realm of righteousness and holiness. There must be a separation of the strength you birth. The church is in trouble today because God has anointed the church with strength; God has anointed the church with grace; God has anointed the church with anointing; but the anointing and the grace and the strength that God has placed on the church have never been sanctified for the work of the Lord. They have never been consecrated, have never been set apart.

One of the requirements before God is able to move in a great and mighty and significant way is that the strength God gives us must be sanctified. It must be consecrated and set aside for the work of the Lord. There has to be a separation. You cannot have the strength of God and use it for your own ends. You have to separate the strength of God. You have to separate the anointing on your life for the work of the Lord.

Numbers 6:1-8:

1 "And the Lord spake unto Moses, saying, 2Speak unto the children of Israel, and say unto them, When either man or woman shall separate themselves to vow a vow of a Nazarite, to separate themselves unto the Lord: 3He shall separate himself from wine and strong drink, and shall drink no vinegar of wine, or vinegar of strong drink, neither shall he drink any liquor of grapes, nor eat moist grapes, or dried. 4All the days of his separation shall he eat nothing that is made of the vine tree, from the kernels even to the husk. 5All the days of the vow of his separation there shall no razor come upon his head: until the days be fulfilled, in the which he separateth himself unto the Lord, he shall be holy, and shall let the locks of the hair of his head grow. 6All the days that he separateth himself unto the Lord he shall come at no dead body. 7He shall not make himself unclean for his father, or for his mother, for his brother, or for his sister, when they die: because the consecration of his God is upon his head. 8All the days of his separation he is holy unto the Lord."

One of the tragedies that have hit the church today is that we have broken the vow of separation. The strengths of the church are not being used for the work of the Lord, but they are being used to fuel the work of the enemy. Samson, who is a type of strength, was a Nazarite. He was consecrated and separated, set aside, for the work of the Lord.

Proverbs 31:1-5:

1 "The words of king Lemuel, the prophecy that his mother taught him. 2What, my son? and what, the son of my womb? and what, the son of my vows? 3Give not thy strength unto women, nor thy ways to that which destroyeth kings. 4It is not for kings, O Lemuel, it is not for kings to drink wine; nor for princes strong drink: 5Lest they drink, and forget the law, and pervert the judgment of any of the afflicted."

In other words, he was warning his son, saying, "Your head is consecrated. You are set aside for the work of the Lord, and because your head is consecrated, give not your strengths, graces, neither your anointing to strange women. Don't waste your strength on that which is immoral. Don't waste your strength on that which is not of God. Do not drink strong wine."

The enemy has infiltrated the church, and because the church has tolerated the enemy, the enemy has gained access and entry. Instead of the church and the leadership giving their strength to the work of the Lord, they have given it to the work of the enemy. We are living in a crucial time. I don't care what anyone says. It's time for the intercessors to rise because the people have a form of godliness, but they deny the power thereof. God is saying it's been going on for too long, and it's time for you to wake up.

Luke 8:17:

"For nothing is secret that shall not be made mainifest; neither anything hid that shall not be known and come abroad."

God says that everything you and I have done in the dark is going to be revealed in the open. The image of jealousy is upon the altar, and what suffers as a result of that is the strength of God.

Ezekiel 8:5:

*Then said he unto me, Son of man, lift up thine eyes now the way toward the north. So I lifted up mine eyes the way toward the north, and behold northward at the gate of the altar this **image** of jealousy in the entry.*

Give not your strength to that which is immoral. As a Nazarite, you are consecrated, you are sanctified, and you are to be righteous and holy. You are to be set aside to do the work of the Lord. What are you doing with the anointing given to you?

The anointing that is supposed to destroy the Philistines is now seducing the Philistines. Manoah's wife sanctified what she birthed and set it aside for the work of the Lord. When the strength is not used in the right way, it generates weakness and finally defeat. When the power is compromised, defeat is inevitable. Samson's strength and anointing were given by God yet were used for his own pleasure.

I'm on the warpath for the kingdom, for the body of Christ. I'm a contender for the faith, and we cannot allow the enemy to come in and destroy us. God will break the bands of barrenness and grant success in every area. But what we don't know is what success will do once it has been birthed. I have said it over and over. It is more difficult to manage success than it is to manage failure.

There are many people who are praying for success, greatness and power, and that's the reason it is important that everyone get a copy of *The Ten Character Tests*. If you don't pass those tests, I guarantee you, when you the limelight your old enemy is going to show up, and it will be too late for you.

Plan to deal with your demons. Deal with the demon in your closet. Deal with your demon while you're in the cocoon. "*I came to blow the trumpet in Zion and sound the alarm in the holy mountain. Let the inhabitants of the land tremble for the day of the Lord is at hand*" (Joel 2:1).

Success has its challenges. Greatness has its challenges. Power has its challenges. It is one thing for you to have success, but how are you going to handle the test and challenges of success? What will power do once it has been given life?

Samson represents anointing unleashed, power released and manifestation of the awesome strength of God revealed. What happens when Samson, which is strength, is birthed, honored and released? Can we handle the authority and power of God, or will we pervert it or let it pervert us? Power has the potential to destroy us if we don't handle it right. Many people who have been destroyed were not destroyed while they were a "nobody." They were destroyed when they became a "somebody."

It is one thing for you to come into the arena of success, but it's another thing to manage that success. Success has its challenges, and there are things that are going to come up against you when you hit the place called success that you never experienced when you were on the ground floor. What happened when Samson's strength was released? If strength is not consecrated, if it is not set apart, if it is not separated for the work of the Lord, it will destroy you.

Samson killed a lion, thirty Philistines and a thousand men, and that's just to name a few. With ease he broke the strongest ropes that were wrapped around him. He carried off the gates of Gaza and destroyed the Temple of Dagon, which was the temple of idolatry. He moved in an unparalleled realm of spiritual power and authority, but his newfound power did not motivate him to conquer his blatant, sinful, sexual relationships with Philistine women.

It's one thing for you to have power and pull down the gates of cities, but if that power cannot be used to pull down the gates of your own heart, something is wrong. The anointing that is given is to destroy yokes and remove burdens. The anointing is given to you so you can cast out devils, lay hands on the sick, raise the dead and more so the anointing initially is given to us to pull down our own demons first.

You cannot say you are anointed and still be struggling with a demon. You cannot say you are anointed and still speak in the tongues of men and the tongues of angels when you know you are still struggling with an issue. What is that anointing doing to deliver you from your own demons? Before you go out and try to deliver other people, first deliver yourself. It is a tragedy with the body of Christ today that many people are out there, trying to deliver everybody else, trying to deliver the world, trying to deliver the nation, but they cannot deliver themselves.

The strength that was birthed to destroy the Philistines was now used to accost and seduce them. God gave the strength to Samson, to pull down the Philistines and destroy them, but Samson used the strength, position, title, power and the influence to seduce the Philistines. God has anointed you to destroy the enemy, but you are using the anointing, the position and the power now to sleep with the enemy.

It's in the body of Christ. The pulpit is polluted, perverted and contaminated. As a result of Samson's self-indulgence after breaking the Nazarite's vow in Judges 16:20, we see the manifestation of *self*-confidence. Everything shifts from God to self, now it's **"I will go out." It's no longer "God will go with me."**

And then we see the manifestation of self-ignorance. You get to the place where the presence of God has left you and you don't even know it. You're just shaking yourself as before. You've got to prophesy like before, but you don't even know the presence of God left you. That is what has been happening in the body of Christ. Many people still have the title, they still have the position, but God is not with them.

Saul was still the king of Israel for forty years, but he was not God's king. The Bible says it took the prophet Samuel. It will take a prophetic voice to rid the kingdom of self-indulgent people who are not using the strength and the power of God to do what God wants them to do.

(3) Self Weakness

The third manifestation is self-weakness. The Philistines laid hands on him.

(4) Self Darkness

The fourth manifestation is self-darkness. They put out Samson's eyes. Now we're in a place whereby we have people who say they can see, but they really cannot see. Their eyes have been put out. They no longer have a vision because they were meddling with the Philistines. See—you need to be able to come back and give an account.

When you have an accident and you go to the hospital, what do the medical people ask you? How did it happen? Where were you when it happened? That's the trouble with us today. There's a lot of stuff happening because you are busy dabbling with the Philistines. You are in the camp of the Philistines. You are in Timnah, you are in Gaza, and you are in Sorek. Nobody knew you were there; but while you were there you lost your faith, you lost your vision, and then you have the audacity to come back and stand before God's people as though you could still see.

(5) Degradation

The fifth manifestation is degradation. The Philistines literally grabbed strength, the anointed man of God, and brought him down to Gaza. They bound him with fetters. The tragedy of it is that many times the Philistines had bound Samson, but each time Samson still had the strength and the anointing to break the bindings with just one sweep. But then he got to a place whereby God was closing in because Samson had broken the Nazarite's vow. He had taken that which was consecrated out from the place of consecration, and instead of using it for the kingdom of God for the body of Christ, he was now using it for the enemy and self gratification.

(6) Self-treachery

We see the sixth manifestation, self-treachery. *"He did grind in the prison house"* (Judges 16:21).

(7) Humiliation

And then we see the seventh manifestation, humiliation in verses 25 and 27 where they called for Samson *"that we may make sport of him, that we may make mockery of him."* This is what happens when we break the vow, when we turn away from being consecrated. This is what happens when we are no longer sanctified and not walking holy. God will allow the devil to humiliate us, and the body of Christ is being mocked and humiliated today by the Philistines.

As God breaks the bands of barrenness He removes the fruitfulness and brings you into another level of temptation and testing. As God provides the grace of enlargement, influence and success you are tempted with an ownership attitude. In other words, you get to a place where you think you own it. You no longer recognize or realize it belongs to God. Now you think the power belongs to you. Just because God has enlarged you and has given you some power, some influence and favor, a nice building, a nice car, a house in a nice neighborhood—now suddenly you forget who actually owns the power. You think the power belongs to you, but the God of the power is getting ready to show you who the power really belongs to.

With the ownership attitude we don't even see God anymore. We don't even pray anymore because now we've become so great and so powerful that we don't need God. As God lends us His power, His strength and anointing, we are tempted to use the power for our own purposes, and we allow a mixture of compromise and blatant disobedience to go unchecked. There is a whole mix so that you don't even know what is real or not real anymore. This is why you need to learn how to seek God for yourself. You need to learn how to fast and pray for yourself. You need to learn how to go and find God for yourself. The arm of flesh will fail you, but God will never fail you.

Stuff goes unchecked because of a name and a title, which one thinks gives them a license to live just any kind of way or do whatever they want to do. We must keep our focus on the God of power rather than the power of God and sanctify the strength for the work of the Lord, the purpose of God.

This message is a turning point. This message will set a paradigm in the lives of the body of Christ. I don't know about you, but I know what it did for me. I was at the feet of God all night because my spirit was heavy. The burden of the Lord was upon me for the body of Christ.

For everything that happens there are casualties. There will always be casualties. That is the reason you've got to watch the choices you make, because your choices carry consequences, and consequences may result in casualties. Someone may be hurt by a choice you've made. You may think it's just you, but it isn't just you because you are connected to people. A lot of times innocent people get hurt because of the choices we make.

So what God is saying is that we've got to sanctify the strength we are birthing for the work of the Lord and for the purpose of God. We've got to sanctify our time and talents for God. We must remember that from now on it's God first. Everything we do is for God. Everywhere we go it's for God. Everything we give is for God. It's God first.

Many things have happened, but must stop and get our eyes off men and personalities and focus on God for our strength. Everything that can be shaken is going to be shaken. This is a wakeup call reminding us to keep eyes fixed on Jesus, the author and the perfecter of your faith (Hebrews 12:1-2).

The only way I can keep praying, praising and worshiping is that I am focused on Jesus.

I am speaking as a trumpet, so hear the clarion call. I am sounding an alarm to the body of Christ. The message is simply this: "*Take your eyes off men and personalities and keep your eyes on Jesus.*" For people who have not learned how to do this, this is the beginning of the great falling away in the body of Christ. Many will fall away as the enemy has hit, and the only reason we have allowed the enemy in is that we have tolerated him.

Revelation 2:20:

...that you have tolerated the harlot Jezebel, the queen and the one who is responsible for sexual immorality and persecution in the body of Christ.

Therefore, it behooves us, the people of God, to rise up now in the spirit of Jehu to annihilate the spirit of Jezebel. Jezebel would like for you to sit on the fence and have a little conversation and discuss it over dinner and talk and talk and talk, but do nothing. But as long as you are a part of the body we are all connected, and it's still going to affect you.

Without Having All the Answers, Believe God

As we get ready to come out of the place of weakness into the place of strength, we must believe God without having all the answers. I don't have all the answers, but I believe God. Even though we may be confused sometimes, we must still believe God, because Romans 3:14 says,

"Let God be true, but every man a liar."

Numbers 23:19 declares, *"Hath he said and shall not do it, or hath he spoken and shall not make it good."*

It doesn't matter what the situation, the surroundings or the circumstances are. It doesn't matter what you are hearing. All you've got to do is believe God, even when you don't have the answers.

Manoah's wife did not know where the angel came from. She didn't know who he was. She just believed God and told her husband. We are living in days when God will speak to us through people we least expect. Can you believe without having all the answers? Manoah and his wife didn't question the messenger, they just believed God. Walking by faith is simply what it means and not by fact. In other words, she knew the practicality of the spiritual. This means that if the spiritual realm is true, then I just believe God for the practicality of that which has already been set in motion in the spiritual realm.

Judges 13:24-25:

24 "And the woman bare a son, and called his name Samson: and the child grew, and the Lord blessed him. 25And the Spirit of the Lord began to move him at times in the camp of Dan between Zorah and Eshtaol."

The strength, which is Samson, began to grow. The anointing began to grow, and the Lord blessed him. *Zorah* means hornet's nest. *Eshtaol* means the place of petition. Now, as the strength, anointing and graces grew, God began to move him between **Zorah, the nest**

of hornets, and **Eshtaol, the place of petition;,** from the nest to petition and prayer. As strength grows, there comes a supernatural movement in the realm of the Spirit as God motivates and provokes you, to challenge you and to move you from the place of the hornet's nest into the place of prayer and petition.

Samson means like the sun. The *sun* is **the** *Son.*

Psalm 84:11:

11 "For the Lord God is a sun and shield: the Lord will give grace and glory: no good thing will he withhold from them that walk uprightly."

The joy of the Lord is our strength. This power begins to manifest itself in the place of prayer, which is Eshtaol, and it is the place of petition. That place of devotion before the Lord, the strength, rises to the place of spiritual warfare. When we are weak, He is strong. When the Spirit moved Samson, he moved from the place of the hornet's nest into the place of prayer and petition. That is what God wants us to do, that even as we are in this time and this season, and especially in the body of Christ, He is desiring us to be moved into the realm of the Spirit from the place of the hornet's nest into the place of prayer and petition.

There are realms and dimensions of prayer, and we have many kinds of prayer. You have prayers of intercession, prayers of supplication, prayers of petition, but God is saying we are now in the time and the season whereby He is requiring us to rise up as intercessors and go into the place of the prayer and petition whereby we are petitioning God to extend mercy, or clemency, to the body of Christ. This is not the time for us to become self-righteous. This is not the time for you to sit down.

1Corinthians 10:12:

"Wherefore let him that thinketh he standeth take heed lest he fall."

In other words, what has happened to one can happen to you. Therefore, the same way you judge, with the same measure you will be judged. This is not the time for you to be pointing fingers or be self-righteous. It is not the time for you and I to exempt ourselves and make ourselves look like we are the Holy Ones of Israel. He that is without sin, let him cast the first stone.

It is time for us to go into the place of prayer and petition whereby we begin to go before God and cry out. This is the time whereby we are doing corporate prayer. It is a prayer of Nehemiah, the prayer of Ezra. It is a prayer whereby we, God's people, confess that we have sinned and fallen short of the glory of God and admit we have strayed from God's righteous ways.

2 Chronicles 7:14:

"If my people, which are called by my name, shall humble themselves, and pray, and seek my face, and turn from their wicked ways; then will I hear from heaven, and will forgive their sin, and will heal their land."

We are weak, but He is strong. We have to get to a place where Samson realized what he had done. He said, (paraphrase) "I broke my vows. I compromised my stand. I released the secret of my strength to my enemies. I lost my sight, lost my vision, lost my perception, lost my relationship with God. I lost my hair (the seven uncut locks symbolizing the uncut covenant relationship with god), lost the anointing, the authority, shook myself like before, but I wist not that the Spirit had departed. I acknowledge my sin." But howbeit that the hair on his head began to grow? (Judges 16:22).

1 John 1:9:

"If we say we have no sin, we deceive ourselves and the truth is not in us"
    but if we confess, He is faithful and He is just to forgive us of all our sins and to cleanse us from all unrighteousness."

I decree that something is growing again. Your strength, anointing, and grace. It is not over until God says it's over. The body of Christ will stand. And we will rise again in the strength of God.

Jeremiah 33:3;

"Call unto me, and I will answer thee, and show thee great and mighty things, which thou knowest not. And Samson called unto the Lord."

Judges 16:28-30:

*28 "And Samson **called** unto the Lord, and said, **O Lord God, remember me, I pray thee, and strengthen me**, I pray thee only this once, O God, that I may be at once avenged of the Philistines for my two eyes. 29And Samson took hold of the two middle pillars upon which the house stood, and on which it was borne up, of the one with his right hand, and of the other with his left. 30And Samson said, Let me die with the Philistines. And he bowed himself with all his might; and the house fell upon the lords, and upon all the people that were therein. **So the dead which he slew at his death were more than they which he slew in his life."***

Oh, Lord, remember Thy people. Remember the souls of men. Remember the people You died for. Oh, Lord, remember us. Strengthen the body. Strengthen the children. Strengthen the men of God. Strengthen the women of God.

Cry out, Zion. Cry out for your sons and daughters. Where are the intercessors? Cry out, Zion. The church will survive, and this too shall pass because we are coming out stronger and we are coming out wiser.

Part 7

And the Lord Remembered Hannah

¹Sing, O barren, thou that didst not bear; break forth into singing, and cry aloud, thou that didst not travail with child: for more are the children of the desolate than the children of the married wife, saith the Lord. ²Enlarge the place of thy tent, and let them stretch forth the curtains of thine habitations: spare not, lengthen thy cords, and strengthen thy stakes; ³for thou shalt break forth on the right hand and on the left; and thy seed shall inherit the Gentiles, and make the desolate cities to be inhabited.—Isaiah 54:1-3

We are literally seeing the manifestation of this word happening in our midst. God is enlarging our tent which is our capacity. We are breaking forth on the right and on the left. The Bible makes us to understand the Word became flesh, and there comes a time when the Word becomes flesh in the midst of the people. God is literally bringing us into a season of enlargement and increase. We are seeing the realization of the Word. When the Word of the Lord comes, it comes to create. I am not just saying this because it sounds good but because we are beginning to see the creativity of this word coming to full manifestation in our lives.

1 Samuel 1:1-3:

1 "Now there was a certain man of Ramathaimzophim, of mount Ephraim, and his name was Elkanah, the son of Jeroham, the son of Elihu, the son of Tohu, the son of Zuph, an Ephrathite: 2 And he had two wives; the name of the one was Hannah, and the name of the other Peninnah: and Peninnah had children, but Hannah had no children. 3 And this man went up out of his city yearly to worship and to sacrifice unto the Lord of hosts in Shiloh. And the two sons of Eli, Hophni and Phinehas, the priests of the Lord, were there."

Now we will talk about Hannah, the womb God used to birth the prophetic kingdom principle. God does not allow anything to happen just for the sake of its happening. Everything God allows has a kingdom agenda. It doesn't matter what season you are in—when you are a child of God He allows you to be in that season because He is going to get the ultimate glory out of it. So now we see here the story of Hannah, the wife of Elkanah who had two wives, Hannah and Peninnah.

Hannah's story takes place during one of Israel's key historical turning points. It was a season whereby a paradigm shift was taking place. There was a changing of order. A new order was being established, and the priesthood was changing. Hannah's birthing of Samuel was very significant, not only in the religious arena, but also in the political arena. There was a changing of the guards, similar to what is happening at this time in our lives.

America is in a time whereby governments are about to change, but likewise what is true in the natural is true in the spirit realm. All truth is parallel. So, as things are changing in the political arena and in the physical arena you and I can see, a paradigm shift is also happening in the religious arena. The priesthood is changing.

Samuel the prophet would be a kingmaker. In the absence of the prophetic being activated in the earth realm Samuel the prophet and judge would lead Israel out of turbulent times in the desert into the prosperous times of the kings. Samuel the prophet would be a kingmaker, a king anointer and a king confronter. The mantle of the anointing of Samuel is an anointing that **makes kings, anoints kings and confronts kings**. It is a very powerful anointing; an anointing that has the Hand of God on it.

Samuel's mother, Hannah, whose name means gracious, would be the foundation for influential ministry to Israel. Again God by His sovereign hand prepared the way for greatness through a barren woman's life of pain, sorrow, rejection and humiliation.

Sometimes God allows us to go through a season of barrenness and unfruitfulness so that He can birth greatness in us. God is about to birth something out of your pain, sorrow, rejection and humiliation. Hallelujah!

Elkanah had two wives, Hannah and Peninnah. Peninnah had children, but Hannah had none. Peninnah was fruitful, productive and lucrative, but Hannah was barren. Peninnah was a type of the flesh, but Hannah was a type of the Spirit. Peninnah produced works of the flesh, according to Galatians 5:19-21. Hannah manifested the fruit of the Spirit, according to Galatians 5:22, which are *"love, joy, peace, longsuffering, gentleness, goodness, faith, meekness and temperance, against which there is no law."*

God wants you to understand the kingdom principle of birthing the fruit of the Spirit even while you are going through your barren and unfruitful season. This is how you know what you are made of when you're going through a season of lack, insufficiency, and unfruitfulness. When it looks like nothing is working for you and when everyone around you is prospering. That is when God brings out the measuring rod and begins to measure your temple to find out where He is in you. (Rev 11)

Do you love Him because of what you have? Do you love Him because of what you can get? Do you love Him because you have a car, a roof over your head or money in the bank? Or do you love Him just because He is God? That's the measure whereby you can tell why people serve God.

What is the reason you serve God? Are you serving God because of His greatness and His power? Or are you serving God simply for the reason that He delivered you from the power of darkness and translated you into the kingdom of His dear Son, in whom you have redemption through the blood, even the forgiveness of sins?

(Colosians 1:10-12) Are you just happy to praise and serve God because you could have been dead and six feet under, but the love of Jesus pulled you out?

If you can only remember where you were and what God did for you that should be enough for you to lift up your voice and praise God. I don't need you to pump me or push me to praise God. It's wonderful to have a praise and worship leader and good music. It's wonderful to have a team backing you up, but you don't really need that if you are a thinking person. Thinking people are thanking people because they remember where God took you from and what He did for them; if you remember how He dried up the tumor in your body. The doctor said you only had six months left to live and Jesus said you shall not die but live and declare the works of God. When you were on the streets and had no money, how He kept you and provided for you.

When you come to a place where you think you are all that and a bag of chips, or you think you are who you are because of your education, your little certificate and your degree, I've come to make an announcement. Without God you are nothing and you can do nothing. You just watch God shut those doors with your certificate and your degree.

One of these two natures, the nature of Hannah and the nature of Peninnah, will dominate us at some point, which is the **flesh and the Spirit** that are always warring against each other. Because Hannah was barren, her rival, Peninnah, provoked her. Therefore, Hannah is an example of the grace of God in the face of disgrace.

Just hold this scripture verse in the back of your mind as we go on.

1 Samuel 2:35:

"And I will raise me up a faithful priest, that shall do according to that which is in mine heart and in my mind: and I will build him a sure house; and he shall walk before mine anointed for ever."

God was saying that the priesthood at that time was not doing what is in my heart and mind, and it is now time for a changing of the guards. This is so powerful. Each and every one of us is called to be a leader in some capacity. Therefore each and every one of us is called to be influential in the kingdom of God, but before that can happen and before that can manifest, the prophetic Word must be birthed in our lives.

Before we birth anything there is always labor, travail and warfare. It's not easy to birth. This is a problem with a lot of people in the church. They labor and labor, and then when they hit the third trimester the pain is so intense they abort. When the pain intensifies, that is the time, the sign and your cue the baby is ready to come forth. The midwives are not going to pity you; they are not going to soothe you and pat you on the back; they are not going to sympathize with you. If you are looking for somebody to comfort you, to feel sorry for you, to tell you exactly what you want to hear, that is the time when the midwife will lock in and tell you to your face that it's too late. You need to bear down and birth this baby.

Likewise, in the kingdom, anytime you get hit from the left and from the right, anytime the pain intensifies, every time the warfare intensifies, every time you feel that all hell has broken loose, that is your sign you are getting ready to birth. Whether the devil likes it or not, whether you believe it or not, it is so and it cannot be otherwise. The only reason I know this to be true is that the warfare has been so intense and the devil extremely overbearing.

There were times when I wanted to give up, but God said the baby was coming. Are you going through the warfare for nothing? Before you can birth anything, there is always going to be labor and travail, and there is always going to be warfare, especially before you birth a new season, a new era and a new move in the earth realm.

1 Samuel 3:1-2:

1 "And the child Samuel ministered unto the Lord before Eli. And the word of the Lord was precious in those days; there was no open vision. 2And it came to pass at that time, when

Eli was laid down in his place, and his eyes began to wax dim, that he could not see; ³and ere the lamp of God went out in the temple of the Lord, where the ark of God was, and Samuel was laid down to sleep; ⁴that the Lord called Samuel: and he answered, Here am I."

First of all, it speaks about the child Samuel. *Samuel* means the name of God. That is what *Sam-U-El* means. God is saying that the name of God is getting ready to be birthed in the church again. We've read about other names that have been birthed in the church, and all these names don't really sound like the name of God, but God is saying He is bringing the body of Christ into a place and into a season where *Sam-U-El*, the name of God, is going to be rebirthed into the kingdom.

Eli was lying down in his place, and his eyes began to wax dim. In other words, in the body of Christ there is a move of God that is beginning to lose its vision. We are coming into a season whereby the former priesthood is beginning to lose its eyes, in other words, their sight, their vision. They are beginning to wax dim to the point that they cannot see.

And it goes on to say the lamp of God went out, referring to the spirit of man which is the candle of the Lord (Proverbs 20:27). The illumination went out in the temple where the ark of God was, but God was right on schedule. God loves His people more than anything else, and there is no way God would leave His people without His presence. There's no way God would leave His people without an anointed leader to carry the next dimension.

God was right on schedule. Before the lamp went out, Samuel was birthed. God always has a man or woman who is next on His agenda or next in line. That is the reason it is important to stay in line so you can be next in line. Don't try to get out because the line is too long. Some of us have missed our season and our visitation because we were impatient and not ready to stay in line.

You are frustrated because the line seems long. You keep looking at the line, wondering where you can jump ahead, but you cannot jump the line. Just stay in line and wait your turn, because you will be next in line if you can only be patient. God always has a man or woman who is next on his agenda. When the King Sauls of a generation disobey Him, God has a David. When the Moses leaders have an attitude, God has a Joshua. When the Vashtis misbehave, He has an Esther. When the twelve disciples tried to compete and monopolize or have vainglory, He had the seventy. When the Elis are weak, He births Samuel. God will never leave His work unfinished. We are birthing the prophetic.

(1) Overcome the Spirit of Peninnah

Before you and I can birth the prophetic we must overcome the spirit of Peninnah. If you have the Spirit of God you always have a worthy portion. Hannah had the Spirit of God. Hannah represented the spirit of God. Peninnah represented the flesh. But if you are of the Spirit of God, you always have a worthy portion or a double portion. You must overcome the spirit of Peninnah.

Every year Elkanah would take his two wives to Shiloh to the temple. These two natures went with Elkanah every year to the temple of God to worship. Do you know that every time you come into the temple of God you are coming in with both natures? Your spirit and your soul are right here, and that's the reason sometimes in church many are in the Spirit, worshiping God, but another group is looking at you and wondering what is going on.

That is the reason when you come to church you need to check your row and make an announcement. You need to be bold enough to look at your row and tell them boldly, "Don't mess up the flow on the whole row. If you can't take the heat, find another seat, because I really came to worship God, and I'm not letting my emotions interrupt my worship. I'm not going to let what I feel right now interrupt my worship." John 4:24 declares, *"God is a Spirit, and they that worship Him must worship Him in Spirit and in truth."*

Peninnah was a type of the flesh. The Bible says Peninnah provoked Hannah daily. The spirit of Peninnah is the spirit of harassment; it's the spirit of mockery, humiliation and embarrassment. "If you say God is with you, why are you barren, why are you infertile, why are you unproductive and why are you unfruitful?"Why is your business not flourishing? Why is your ministry not prospering? Why are you jobless, broke and busted? You are in church five days a week; you fast, you pray, you are on the board of every department. So if you say God is with you why aren't you gratified? The spirit of Peninnah is alive and well even in the Church.

You need to shut the mouth of Peninnah. The spirit of Peninnah will fill your heart with sorrow and guilt. It makes you question your calling, maybe even your relationship with God. The spirit of Peninnah will harrass you to the point where you think you're not saved, you're not born again, and you're not a child of God. Why? Because the spirit of Peninnah is the spirit of torture, harassment and provocation. Hannah's rival, Peninnah, made her miserable. That spirit is meant to break your spirit, but don't let Peninnah get to you.

There are two kinds of barrenness. There's a natural barrenness, and there's a spiritual barrenness. The spiritual barrenness comes when God shuts your womb. If God shuts it, then we understand it's only for a season, because He's a God who will shut doors no man can open. Isaiah 22:22;

"God will open a door, and no man can shut it."

The Lord had shut Hannah's womb. Yet the spirit of Peninnah always looks for our weak spot and hits, taunts, annoys and provokes us. That's what Peninnah did. Peninnah knows exactly what to do to break your defenses, to make you feeble, to cause you not to pray. *To provoke* means to put into inward commotion, to confuse or torment. We must shut Peninnah's mouth.

(2) Recognize the Spirit
Before you and I can birth the prophetic we must discern and recognize that spirit even in the church. The Bible says year after year Elkanah took both Hannah and Peninnah to Shiloh to the temple. A lot of the provocation from Peninnah came while they were in the temple.

1 Samuel 1:7:

"And as he did so year by year, when she went up to the house of the Lord, so she provoked her; therefore she wept, and did not eat."

The spirit of Peninnah is a spirit that will provoke you to weeping and the loss of your appetite. Satan's attack and timing are calculated. They are strategized and directed to specific times and places. Satan provokes us at the time when we should be enjoying God's presence, celebrating God's victory and ministering to others in the house of the Lord. The attack most times is on our own ground, our place of prayer and worship, our churches and ministries.

The more Elkanah showed his love for Hannah and gave her a double portion, the more Peninnah provoked her. The more God loves us, comforts us and encourages us, the more the enemy taunts us. You come to church full of faith and love for God, believing and trusting God, waiting for your king to come, and then the spirit of Peninnah will ask a stupid question like "How old are you now, and you're still not married?" Or, "When did you lose your job again? You still haven't got a job?"

You have to be able to recognize it as a spirit. The spirit of Peninnah will provoke you while you are in the presence of God. You come to worship and praise God and fellowship, but then here comes the spirit of Peninnah. The reason Peninnah shows up at that particular time is to ruffle your spirit. You cannot worship God effectively when your spirit is torn up. The spirit of Peninnah will choose the time.

Just when you are getting ready to connect with heaven, the spirit of Peninnah will ask you a stupid question or make a stupid comment. "Oh, did you sing that song? I liked it better when So-and-So sang it." I want you to recognize the spirit of Peninnah. Don't let that spirit shift your focus. You must be able to look that spirit in the face and make a declaration: "For God I live, and for God I die. I didn't come here to worship you. I came to worship the true and living God. I refuse to be distracted."

We must learn to recognize, appreciate and honor one another. It doesn't matter what we do. You do what you do, and I do what I do, but we need one another. We are not here to compete. We are here to compliment God. The anointing will make us agree with one another.

You have to be able to recognize the spirit. Peninnah comes to church, dressed up in a suit, shiny shoes, wig and a phony pony. You have to be able to recognize it because Luke 6:45 says that *"out of the abundance of the heart the mouth speaks."* Your words are ambassadors. It is your words that will betray you. I don't know what you're thinking until you open your mouth. When you open your mouth I know what kind of spirit is in you. Recognize the spirit of Peninnah and shut it down. Romans 8:31 declares, *"If God be for me, who can be against me?"* Don't intimidate me or manipulate me. Don't make me feel less than who I am.

(3) Stay in the Spirit

Before you can birth the prophetic in your life, you've got to be able to stay in the spirit. 1 Samuel 1:8 the Bible says Elkanah asked Hannah three questions, which represent the body, the soul and the spirit. Elkanah asked Hannah was, "

a. *Why weepest thou?"* That has to do with your soul your will and your emotions.
b. *"Why eatest thou not?"* That has to do with your body, the flesh.
c. *"Why is thy heart grieved?"* That has to do with your spirit, because your spirit is always attached to your heart.

This is the threefold nature of man, and there is a difference among the three, especially between the soul and the spirit.

Hebrews 4:12: *"For the word of God is quick, and powerful, and sharper than any two-edged sword, piercing even to the dividing asunder of soul and spirit."*

1Thessalonians 5:23 the Bible says, *"I pray God your whole spirit and soul and body be preserved blameless unto the coming of our Lord Jesus Christ."*

Therefore, there are two different realms. The spirit realm is a dimension of man which deals with the spiritual realm, so man deals with God in his spirit. That is the God realm. The soul realm is the dimension of man that deals with the mental realm. It deals with man's intellect, the sensibilities, feelings, the emotions and the will, the part that reasons and thinks.

That is why you cannot serve God with your soul or with what you feel. "Well, I don't feel like it because I was offended, so I'm not going to church." You're a phony. "She stepped on my toes, so I'm not going to serve God." Are you serving God, or are you serving man? You are serving God from your soulish area.

Your body is the dimension that deals with the physical realm. It deals with your fleshly appetites. God is not going to do anything with our bodies or our minds. If you are in the flesh, God won't do anything. He will not do business with you.

Romans 7:18:

"...because in this flesh dwells no good thing."

And God is not going to do anything with us based on our soulish emotions. So you can cry all you want, but God isn't listening. He doesn't deal with you based on your emotions. He doesn't deal with you based on your flesh.

This is why some people are offended with God and with leadership, because they are constantly in the flesh and in their soulish area. Your spirit is constantly waging war against your soul. The carnal mind is the enemy of God, and because you are in the flesh your flesh gets offended. If you are in the spirit your feelings won't get hurt, because it would have been the Spirit ministering to your spirit. The preacher does not preach to your flesh, but to your spirit. Your spirit is the one that is connected to God. If you serve God, you must serve Him by your spirit.

Romans 1:9:

For God is **my** *witness, whom* **I** **serve** **with** **my** **spirit** *in the gospel of his Son, that without ceasing I make mention of you always in* **my** *prayers;*

God will not respond to anything that we do with our bodies or our minds. God has a contract with our spirits. When you and I were born again, it was our spirits that were regenerated. I never saw anybody who gave his life to the Lord Jesus Christ and suddenly had an instant facelift. Your face looks exactly the same, and you're wearing the same clothes, but there is a spiritual transformation that took place, because it was your spirit that got regenerated. That's the reason you can get born again right now and still go out there and physically sin. In your flesh.

The salvation of God is three dimensional. It is the spirit that gets born again first, and then you are delivered, are being delivered and will be delivered again (2 Corinthians 1:10). The last part that will be delivered is the flesh. That's why children of God filled with the Holy Spirit who speak in the tongues of men and the tongues of angels can still walk out of church and go fornicate, and yet your spirit is born again.

So after you are born-again, fire-baptized and Holy Ghost-filled, we have the responsibility to do something with our bodies. God is not going to come and do something about your body. He has already done His part, which was to regenerate your spirit and reconcile you back unto Himself.

Romans 12:1

"present your body as a living sacrifice... "

God didn't say *He* would present it. *You* must present it. Do something about your body. The preacher cannot do anything about your body. The apostles cannot do anything about your body. You have the responsibility to do something about your body. Put the reins on your body. Control your appetites, and present your body as a living sacrifice, holy and acceptable unto God.

God will not do anything with your mind. God doesn't even have control over your mind. If God had control over your mind, some of you would not be doing the stuff you do. Some of you wouldn't be thinking the things you think. That just shows you God has no control over your mind. You must do something with your mind. Paul tells us in Roman 12:2 to be transformed by the renewing of our minds. Put on the mind of Christ.

Our minds are renewed by two methods:

(1) feedi upon God's Word in your own private study and meditation daily,
(2) Spirit-anointed teachers the five-fold ministry (Ehesians 6).

When you present your body and renew your mind you will connect to the Spirit, work in the Spirit, live in the Spirit and stay in the Spirit.

(4) Pray Out and Pour Out
We are birthing the prophetic.

1 Samuel 1:10:

*10"And she was in bitterness of soul, and **prayed unto the Lord**, and wept sore." Now look at verse 15: 15"And Hannah answered and said, No, my lord, I am a woman of a sorrowful spirit: I have drunk neither wine nor strong drink, but have **poured out** my soul before the Lord."*

Before you can birth the prophetic you've got to **pray** and **pour** out, that's point number four. Hannah was in bitterness of soul. Her emotions, her feelings, her sensibilities were hurt because of the torment, the harassment and the provocation of the enemy, Bitterness, anger and resentment had crept in.

I cannot stand Christians who pretend and say things like, "Well, you know what, I'm fine. I'm a child of God. Nothing's wrong with me. They can do whatever they want. I don't care." No. You are a liar. You do care because, you must remember, you are a trichotomy. You are a body, a soul and a spirit. Your spirit may not be hurt, but it's your soul, your emotions, your feelings, your sensibilities.

The enemy can't touch your spirit, the Spirit of God is regenerating your spirit. It's the soulish man, your emotions, your feelings, your desire area, that was hurt. And because your feelings were hurt, a portal was opened that allowed in bitterness, anger, resentment. You've got to **pray and pour out**. It's not enough just to pray and not pour out. You've got to pour out and pray. That is why in your prayer time you have to empty yourself, because you are not too holy to not have some kind of residue in there.

You may have had great expectations. You just knew you were going to get that job, but you ended up not getting it. You are human enough to be hurt. There is an area in you that will be disappointed, and the enemy will use that to plant the root of bitterness.

Hannah was in bitterness of soul. Her feelings and emotions and sensibilities were hurt because of the torment, the harassment and the provocation of the enemy. Bitterness and resentment had crept in. So she prayed and poured out, and she poured out and prayed. This kind of prayer is intense prayer. It is deep prayer, hot prayer. She poured out her anger, her resentment, her bitterness, her unforgiveness, her sorrow, embarrassment, shame and reproach. She emptied herself.

If I don't like what you said to me I'm going to pour it out at the altar; if I regard iniquity in my heart, Psalm 66:18 declares that God will not hear me. You can't go around contaminated and polluted because somebody hurt you two years ago. The Bible says that if you harbor anything against your brother go to him. How is he going to know he offended you unless you give him the opportunity and the benefit of the doubt? Give him a platform to explain himself. He probably offended you unknowingly.

You are carrying all this in your body, your system is polluted. It is contaminated because of the root of bitterness. The Bible warns in Hebrews 12:15 not to allow the root of bitterness to spring up. We must pray and pour out. Pour out and pray. It was a prayer that was birthed out of Hannah's distress. She prayed earnestly and passionately. Hannah was not intoxicated with strong drink, but she was intoxicated with a deep burden of prayer. Only her lips moved, according to Romans 8:26.

Sometimes you have such a burden that only your lips are moving, and the Bible says the Spirit Himself makes intercession for us with groanings that cannot be uttered. I'm talking about when you are so burdened with the weight of the world and you are coming into prayer on your knees. Nothing is coming out of your mouth, but your lips are moving. Why? Because out of your pain, out of your vexation, out of your agony, out of your anger, all you can do is just move your lips. It's not to impress anybody. It's not to look important. It's between you and God when you are getting ready to empty yourself. God wants to fill that empty space when it is poured out with something that is powerful, something that is prophetic, something that will be a kingmaker, something that will be a king anointer, something that will be a king confronter. Even the anointing of Samuel, the name of God, is about to be birthed out of your pain.

(5) Make a Vow to God

There comes a time in our lives when we've tried everything. We've done all we know to do and things are still not happening. This is now the time to make a vow to God. Hannah had tried everything, but nothing seemed to be working so she took it to the next level. In 1 Samuel 1:11 she made a vow to God. A vow is a solemn promise or statement. If a vow is made it is as sacredly binding as any oath, according to Deuteronomy 23:21-23.

Hannah's vow was a reflection of the depths of her despair and her brokenness. She vowed she would give up ownership completely and give back her son exclusively for God's use. You have to come to a point where you make an oath to God that if He gives it to you; you vow to give up ownership of it. If you want it for the wrong reason, because you want to be able to say you own it, so you can show off to your friends and use it as proof that God is with you, or you want it so you can prove to Peninnah that God loves you too, He will not give it to you.

But Hannah came to a point where she gave up ownership. She said to God, "If You give it to me I'm giving it back to You. If You bless me I'm going to give the blessing right back to You, because I understand it doesn't really belong to me."

Do you understand that nothing you have really belongs to you? Not even your children belong to you. They came through you, but they are not for you. You were just the birth canal that brought them into the earth realm. The children belong to God. You are just a steward over what really belongs to God. So Hannah took the next step to birthing the prophetic, and she gave up ownership if He gave him to her. She gave her son exclusively for God's use.

I remember my husband always said every one of our children were given back to God, every last one of the seven. They don't belong to us; they belong to God, and that's the reason you see them serving God. They have no choice but to serve in the temple of God, because we gave them back to God. When I was pregnant I remember my husband praying and saying, "Lord, I give this child back to You. Use him for Your glory." When you give up ownership and say to God, "If You give it to me I'm giving it back to You," it moves something in the Spirit.

A lot of times when you talk about vows, it relates to money, and yes, sometimes you need to make a monetary vow if you are desperate for God to move in a certain way. I have often made a monetary vows to God. "If You do this for me, this is what I'm going to present at Your altar." I'm just that desperate for this thing to break in the realm of the Spirit. It's a dimension I'm looking for God to break through for me, and I made a vow between me and God, saying, "If You do it for me, God, I will bring it to the temple of the Lord, and I will thank You for what You have done for me." And God has always come through.

So yes it can be in monetary terms, but it relates also to everything. In other words, you have to get to a point where you vow to God that, if He does it for you, you will do it for Him. "If You give me a son I'll give him back to You." "If You save me I will serve You all the days of my life." "If You bless me financially, God, I will feed the poor; I will help the less fortunate; I will support the church." "If You give me a husband I will give him back to You." "If You give me a ministry I will give it back to You." Our bishop says all the time this ministry is not ours. This ministry does not belong to Sarah Morgan or Peter Morgan. This ministry belongs to God.

Malachi 3:10 says that when you give it back to Him, God opens the portals of heaven and releases a blessing you will not be able to contain.

(6) Touch and Agree with Leadership

This is a very powerful kingdom principle many people have missed. It is in 1 Samuel 1:17:

"Then Eli answered and said, Go in peace: and the God of Israel grant thee thy petition that thou hast asked of him." Hannah got to the place where she went to Eli, the high priest. Even though Eli's lamp was beginning to go out, a little trickle of anointing was still there, and because Hannah followed divine protocol God honored Eli's decree.

A priest was a mediator. One authorized to perform the sacred rites of a religion especially as a mediatory agent between humans and God. Even though we are able to go to Christ for ourselves, there are certain things in your life that will not break without the intervention of a priest (Leviticus 4:20-35, 5:10). You need an anointing of the priesthood to intervene on your behalf. Once the priest intervenes on your behalf, there is an anointing; there is a dimension, a realm that God honors, because the anointing is on the head. So, when the anointing goes before God on your behalf, God has no choice but to hear and to break forth that thing in your life.

Mediation, mediator: *the activity and person performing it of functioning as a go-between or intermediary between two people or parties, in order to initiate a relationship, promote mutual understanding or activity, or effect a reconciliation after a dispute.* In the study of religion mediation usually refers to a person who represents the community in worship and other contacts with divine beings. In the Old Testement various figures in Israel's history mediate between God and humans and in the nt Jesus is the unique mediator who reconciles sinful humans to God.

In the Old Testament the priests are religious mediators between humans and God. Their functions include offering community and private sacrifices, praying and singing in the Temple, protecting the integrity of the holy places and rituals, and maintaining themselves in a state of ritual purity. All the religious regulations concerning priests, holy places, worship, and the Temple were designed to render humans holy so that they could relate to a God who is holy. The priests themselves were consecrated to their special office (Exod. 29; Lev. 8) as mediators between the profane and the holy. Priests also blessed the people (Num. 6:22-27) and offered the first fruits brought to the Temple by the people (Deut. 26:1-10). The mediating function of the priesthood can be seen most clearly on the Day of Atonement, when the high priest alone entered the Holy of Holies, the inner chamber of the Temple, to offer incense in atonement for all the sins of the people during the past year (Num. 16).

Major Old Testament leaders also mediated between God and Israel. Abraham sacrificed and prayed to God in the name of his clan (Gen. 12:7-8) and he also interceded on behalf of Sodom and Gomorrah (Gen. 18:22-33). Jacob sacrificed to God and received God's blessing on all his descendants in Israel (Gen. 35:1-15). Moses mediated between God and the Hebrews in Egypt, during the wandering in the desert, at Sinai, and when Israel sinned by worshiping the golden calf (Exod. 32:30-34). Joshua mediated between God and the people in the making of the covenant in Israel (Josh. 24:14-28), Samuel mediated the appointment of the first king (1 Sam. 8-12), and Solomon prayed in the people's name at the dedication of the Temple (1 Kings 8:22-53). The prophets who acted as God's messengers in bringing his word to the people also acted as mediators in effecting reconciliation between the people and God (Jer. 14:1-9). Finally, the Suffering Servant found in Second Isaiah 53, whatever his identity, atones for the sins of Israel and effects a reconciliation between God and Israel.

In the New Testament Jesus is explicitly called a mediator in only four passages, one from the Pauline literature and three from Hebrews. "*For there is one God, and there is one mediator between God and men, the man Christ Jesus, who gave himself as a ransom for all*" (1 Tim. 2:5-6). In Hebrews Christ is three times said to mediate the new covenant between God and humans (Heb. 8:6; 9:15; 12:24). Hebrews also develops a notion that is found in the passage from 1 Timothy, namely, that Jesus redeems humans. All these statements in Hebrews are set in the context of the new temple in heaven where Christ is the high priest and the one perfect sacrifice. Jesus also mediates by praying for his disciples (John 17; Matt. 11:25-27), by healing, by teaching God's word, and by forgiving people their sins. All Jesus' activities to save humans can be looked on as mediation between God and humanity (though the New Testament does not use that category to characterize Jesus' work and words). Consequently, believers are instructed to pray in Jesus' name to God (John 14:13). Many Pauline and Gospel passages say or imply that contact with God is through Jesus Christ and this implies mediation by Jesus. A.J.S.

Numbers 16:46-50:

46And Moses said unto Aaron, Take a censer, and put fire therein from off the altar, and put on incense, and go quickly unto the congregation, and make an atonement for them: for there is wrath gone out from the LORD; the plague is begun. 47And Aaron took as Moses commanded, and ran into the midst of the congregation; and, behold, the plague was begun among the people: and he put on incense, and made atonement for the people. 48And he stood between the dead and the living; and the plague was stayed. 49Now they that died in the plague were fourteen thousand and seven hundred, beside them that died about the matter of Korah. 50And Aaron returned unto Moses unto the door of the tabernacle of the congregation: and the plague was stayed.

Hebrews 2:17-18:

"Wherefore in all things it behooved him to be a merciful and faithful high priest in things (pertaining) to God to make reconciliation for the sins of the people. 18 For in that He Himself hath suffered.

Hebrews 4:14:

Seeing then that we have a great high priest, that is passed into the heavens, Jesus the Son of God, let us hold fast [our] profession.

Based on these scripture references we see that God has always had a priest/mediator in the earth.

One of the issues we have in the church today, especially the twenty-first-century church, is that we have a generation of people, according to Proverbs 26:12, who are wise in their own eyes. We can fast for ourselves; we can pray for ourselves, we can read the Bible for ourselves and I can go on the internet and whip up a sermon for myself. Anybody can go on the internet and borrow messages, but do you have a revelation? Do you have something that during a time of fasting and prayer God has birthed in your spirit?

Hannah honored the protocol. She said to God, "I can't do this for myself. I need the intervention of the priest." The Bible says that when she did that Eli said, "Go in peace, and may the Lord grant you your desire."

(7) Worship Before the Lord

1 Samuel 1:19-20:

*19 "And they rose up in the morning early, and **worshipped** before the Lord, and returned, and came to their house to Ramah: and Elkanah knew Hannah his wife; and the Lord remembered her. 20Wherefore it came to pass, when the time was come about after Hannah had **conceived**, that she bare a son, and called his name Samuel, saying, Because I have asked him of the Lord."*

Conception takes place in **worship**. Now we're talking about two different realms because anybody can praise God. Praise is outer court. That's the place where everybody is—the saved and not saved. That's praise. Some know Jesus, and some don't know Jesus.

They do what you do, jump for joy, clap their hands. Praise is outer court; it's for everybody. That's what the Bible says in Revelation 11:1-2. It says to take the measuring rod and measure the temple, but don't measure the outer court where the dogs are. Psalm 150 says, "*Let* everything *that has breath praise the Lord.*"

In the outer court you are praising God for what you have, what you can see, what you can touch, and you are just praising God because He gave you a new car, because you've got money in the bank, you have a man in your bed, you bought a new pair of shoes. You are thanking God for all the petty stuff. "Thank You, God. I had enough money to do my nails." "Thank You, God. I have enough gas in my car." "Thank You, God, for putting food on my table." That's all outer court stuff, and there's nothing wrong with that because the Bible says to let everything that has breath praise God. But worship goes to another level, another dimension. That's where the plumb line is. That's the measure right there to see who are the real worshipers. Key number seven is to worship before the Lord.

I'm afraid of people who are afraid to get intimate with God, people who are afraid to lock in and break down in the presence of God and let their tears roll down and just love God for who He is. It tells me volumes about who they are. The word *worship* there comes from the word *shachah.* It means to prostrate yourself, to bow down, to worship, to lie down and go before God. It means to pay homage, to reverence Him.

We praise Him for what we see. We worship Him for who He is. To worship Him you must get to a place where you go to God and say, "God, if I never have a car, if You never heal me, if You never deliver me, You are God, the only living God, the only sovereign God, ever living, ever giving. You are the only God, and it doesn't matter whether You do it or not. I'll worship You because You are God. You are Elohim; You are Yahweh; You are Adonai; You are the King of kings and the Lord of lords, the great I Am. You are alpha and omega, the beginning and the end. You are the first and the last. You are my mountain mover, my burden bearer, my yoke destroyer, my kinsman redeemer, my ever-present help in time of trouble. You are my rock. You are my fortress. You are my deliverer." When you worship, go before Him and lie prostrate and just lie there in His presence.

"I have no money, but You are God."

"My marriage is in trouble, but You are God."

"Everything around me is falling apart, but You are God."

If you are in your car, you can begin to worship. If you are broke, busted and disgusted, you can still acknowledge Him as God. Lift your hands in worship. Don't let anything interfere with your worship. Conception takes place in worship. That is when the atmosphere is tame, when the place becomes conducive, when you tell God how much He means to you.

"And Elkanah knew (was intimate with) Hannah his wife; and the Lord remembered her, and she conceived." As God remembered Hannah so shall He remember you. Sing, O barren, for you shall conceive and birth your Samuel which is the prophetic.

Part 8

Elizabeth

¹Sing, O barren, thou that didst not bear; break forth into singing, and cry aloud, thou that didst not travail with child: for more are the children of the desolate than the children of the married wife, saith the Lord. ²Enlarge the place of thy tent, and let them stretch forth the curtains of thine habitations: spare not, lengthen thy cords, and strengthen thy stakes; ³ for thou shalt break forth on the right hand and on the left; and thy seed shall inherit the Gentiles, and make the desolate cities to be inhabited.—Isaiah 54:1-3

God has extracted some very powerful kingdom principles out of this one particular Scripture passage as we have been examining the seven barren wombs God used to birth seven kingdom principles in the earth realm. Now we will examine the womb of Elizabeth that brought forth John the Baptist, which is symbolic of the principle of **repentance** and **preparation**. The predominant quality God wants us to bring forth is **Jesus, the perfection and the completion of all things.** Luke 1:5-7:

5"There was in the days of Herod, the king of Judea, a certain priest named Zacharias, of the division of Abijah. His wife was of the daughters of Aaron, and her name was Elizabeth. 6And they were both righteous before God, walking in all the commandments and ordinances of the Lord blameless. 7But they had no child, because Elizabeth was barren, and they were both well advanced in years."

Please remember those names because, as we continue, you will see they carry great significance. We have Zacharias of the division of Abijah and his wife, a daughter of Aaron, whose name was Elizabeth, and she was barren because they were both advanced in age.

All the other wombs we have discussed were in the Old Testament, and this is our first New Testament barren womb. You may think that was just for Old Testament times, that God doesn't do that in the New Testament, which is the new covenant; however, the principles of God still remain the same.

Principles are the principal thing. God is no respecter of persons. God is a respecter of principles; when the enemy raises his hand or comes in like a flood, and the Spirit of the Lord raises up a standard on your behalf, you cannot use your emotions to fight the enemy. This is when the principles of the Word of God come into play. When you have an understanding of what the Word of God has birthed in your spirit, then you are able to pull out your principles and wage war intelligently against the onslaught of the enemy.

This account of the womb of Elizabeth is found in the New Testament in the days of Herod, the king of Judea. The Bible says a certain priest named **Zacharias, whose name means Jehovah has remembered**, or **concentrating on Jehovah**, was of the division of Abijah. When you study the book of Chronicles you will see that when the priesthood came into reign through Aaron there was a dividing of the priesthood into divisions according to their duties.

The Bible says in 1 Chronicles 24:6-19 that there were twenty-four priestly divisions in the entire priesthood. In other words, there were assigned duties. They had a roster whereby they would be required to come and perform their priestly duties. Each division or section was required to serve at the temple for one week twice a year. There were twenty-four divisions, which were the division of Aaron, the division of Eleazar, and all the others who were a part of the Zadokite priesthood.

Their duties were divided or assigned by lot, and Abijah was assigned the **eighth division**, according to 1 Chronicles 24:10. **The number eight is the number of new beginnings**. So Abijah was out of the division in which Zacharias served, which was the eighth division, indicating a new beginning. Something new was getting ready to happen.

The name Zacharias means Jehovah has remembered. His wife was Elizabeth, the descendant of Aaron, the brother of Moses. Aaron was a high priest, so Elizabeth had come out of good stock. Today Elizabeth would be called a PK, a pastor's kid. She had a good spiritual pedigree. There was good blood running in the veins of Elizabeth. She grew up in the church, grew up around church folk, grew up watching her father perform his priestly duties. She saw people bringing their sacrifices to God and all of that so Elizabeth had a knowledge of the God her father grew up serving. The name *Elizabeth* **means God is my oath, or God has promised me.**

As we progress in this particular study, I want you to have in the back of your spirit that it doesn't matter what it looks like, seems like, sounds like; it doesn't matter what the enemy is whispering into your spirit. There is one thing you must know, **God has remembered and God has promised something.**

There's something about having a promise from God that makes you resolute in your spirit. There is something about having a promise from God that will help you to "take a lickin' and keep on tickin'." There's something about having a promise from God that will enable you to stand in the midst of adversity, because you have a promise and an assurance that God is a God of remembrance. You may not remember me, but one thing about God, *He* has a long memory.

Malachi 3:16:

16Then they that feared the LORD spake often one to another: and the LORD hearkened, and heard it, and a book of remembrance was written before him for them that feared the LORD, and that thought upon his name. 17And they shall be mine, saith the LORD of hosts, in that day when I make up my jewels; and I will spare them, as a man spareth his own son that serveth him. 18Then shall ye return, and discern between the righteous and the wicked, between him that serveth God and him that serveth him not.

Many times we are looking to people to remember what we've done for them, how we've been there for them, how we've prayed for them. I want you to know that sometimes people will forget you, but God will never forget you. We are told in Malachi 3:16 that there is a **book of remembrance**. A time and a season comes when God requires the book of remembrance to be brought out, and when He opens the book of remembrance every prayer you've prayed has been recorded.

Every petition, every supplication, every request you've made before God has been recorded in the book of remembrance, and when God draws open the book of remembrance, God will reward you according to the measure of the deposit you have made. Every good work that you have done, every bit of help you have extended to someone, every sacrifice you have made out of your way, Malachi 3:16-18 says God has recorded it in a book of remembrance.

Hebrews 6:10:

For God is not unrighteous to forget your work and labour of love, which ye have shewed toward his name, in that ye have ministered to the saints, and do minister.

This the reason you don't need to trip when people forget about you. At the end of the day people are just a resource, but God is the source. So whether you ever remember me or not, one thing is certain, God is a God of remembrance. There are many times and seasons when we begin to wonder, "God, have You forgotten me?" I love that song that says, "I am not forgotten. God knows my name." As long as God knows your name, God is going to remember you.

Elizabeth had a promise from God and would do anything to hold on until that promise came to pass. There is one thing I know without a shadow of doubt, God can do anything but lie. God continually admonishes us. He said when you get to that place whereby you have an understanding about the ways of God, let all men be liars, but let God be true. The Bible says that to the children of Israel God showed His acts, but to His servant Moses He showed His ways. (Psalm 103)

Please understand. It is important for you to know the ways, the method, the means of how God operates, rather than just looking for the acts of God. Long after the acts have ceased, the ways of God will sustain you.

There came a time and a season when the miracles ceased, but it was the ways, the principles, the means, and the methods of God that were able to sustain the people of God. So when you have an understanding of the **ways** of God, then you are not easily swayed to the right or to the left. It doesn't matter how bad it looks; it doesn't matter how intense it is; it doesn't matter how much you are being pressed from every side; there's *something* you know about God. That sustains and undergirds you.

That is the reason a man like Job was able to stand in the midst of his trial because he knew something the other people did not know. Job used a very powerful word when he said, *"Behold I go forward, but he is not there; and backward but I cannot perceive him: On the left hand, where he doth work, but I cannot behold him: he hideth himself on the right hand that I cannot see him"* (Job 23:8-9). In other words, he was speaking about the **manifest** presence of God, but then he went on to say, in verse 10, *"The Lord knows the way that I take, and when he has tried me, I will come forth as gold."* He said, "It doesn't matter what it seems like; it doesn't matter what it looks or sounds like; it doesn't matter what's going on in my body. My skin has clung to my bones. I am ashamed and have become a reproach to everyone who knew me, but there is one thing I know. I know my Redeemer lives, and I will see Him not in my grave, but in this life."(Job 19:25)

Please understand. There's a difference between just believing and knowing. It's one thing for you to believe, but it's another thing for you to move to the next dimension, which is the dimension of knowing—in other words, convinced beyond compromise.

Daniel said in Daniel 11:32 that the people who know their God shall be strong and do great exploits. Romans 8:38-39:

38 "For I am persuaded, that neither death, nor life, nor angels, nor principalities, nor powers, nor things present, nor things to come, 39nor height, nor depth, nor any other creature, shall be able to separate us from the love of God, which is in Christ Jesus our Lord."

It's not just about believing: I love it when people say they believe God. But do they know Him? Do you know Him to the point that even when something is dead and He shows up, it has no choice but to live again? There is a dimension, a place in God, where you go past just believing. You have such an encounter with God that every fiber of your being knows Him in a way that other people don't know Him. That's the place where it doesn't matter what anyone says, and you are able to look in their faces and say, "For God I die, and for God I live."

Zacharias and Elizabeth knew Him. The Bible says in Luke 1:6 that they were both righteous people and they were blameless. They were in right standing with God. They were good people. They were virtuous and moral. They were worthy and irreproachable and honorable people. In other words, they were genuinely godly, walking in the commandments and the ordinances of God, blameless. If it were today we would say they were saved for real.

Are you saved for real? You know, some of us are just saved on Sunday, but we're not saved the rest of the week. But the Bible says these two were saved for real (paraphrase). In other words, you're not just saved on Sunday; you're saved at your job, while you're riding the bus, while walking down the street, while you're in the mall. Are you saved for real?

They were saved for real. Not half-saved folk or quarter-saved folk, where they are saved in the church service and then they're sinning in the parking lot. These people were saved for real. But the Bible says in Luke 1:7 that they had no children. They were unfruitful; they were unproductive because Elizabeth was barren.

(1) Stay At Your Post

Zacharias and Elizabeth were saved and righteous; they were holy and blameless, serving God and walking according to the commandments of God. They paid their tithes and offerings. They never missed a Sunday service; they never missed a Bible study and never missed prayer meeting. They were there because their whole lives were to serve God, but in spite of all of that they were barren.

Do you know someone like this? Have you ever been there? When you know you are doing what is right for God? You are serving Him the way you are supposed to serve Him; you are living right; you are walking right; you are not fooling around; you aren't dipping and diving, slipping and sliding. You read your Bible every day. You pray every day. You are on your floor every morning at five a.m., and you are seeking the face of God.

You have the tools available on prayer such as *Rules of Engagement, Commanding Your Morning,* by my friend Dr. Cindy Trimm and you've been applying those rules every day of the year, and yet it looks like nothing is happening.

Before you can birth repentance and preparation you have to keep serving and **stay at your post**. Many years ago I gave a message called "Provoking Your Angel." It came out of this same text.

The Bible says in Luke 1:8 that it came to pass while Zacharias was serving—*while* **he was serving**—not before, not after, but *while* he was at his post, *while* he was on duty. In other words, he did not allow his circumstance to deter him from his assignment. In spite of the fact that they were barren—and they knew they were faithful, committed, righteous, blameless and yet barren—they continued to serve faithfully. The keyword there is *while*, in the course of.

In other words, I'm going to do what I'm supposed to do. I'm not going to sit back and have a pity party because I don't know when my visitation will come. The name *Zacharias* **means the Lord remembers**, and the name *Elizabeth* **means my God is an absolutely faithful One, or my God is an oath or promise keeper.** Therefore, I choose to trust God as the faithful God who remembers all His promises to us and for us. I will not be moved by this season of barrenness, infertility and unproductivity. I will keep serving according to my division. I'll be at my post every time the doors of the church are open because I don't know when God will choose to visit me.

You don't know what day, what hour or what moment God will choose to give you a breakthrough. Many times we have missed our breakthrough because we were not at our post. The day God chose to show up, to bless us and give us our breakthrough was the day we decided we were too tired to be at our post. But Zacharias continued to serve God in spite of his situation, his age and what people said.

I will keep serving according to my division. I will be at my post every time the door of my church is open. If I'm an usher I'll keep ushering. If I'm a musician I'll keep playing my instrument. If I'm a singer I'm going to keep singing. If I'm a teacher I'll keep teaching. If I'm an altar worker I'll keep catching. If I'm a preacher I'll keep preaching. If I'm an intercessor I'll keep praying. If I'm a giver I'm going to keep giving. Why? Because God is a God of remembrance.

Stay at your post, because God gave you a promise and God remembers. Zacharias was still serving and going about his priestly duties. Job said, "All the days of my appointed time I will wait till my change comes." The extraordinary happens on an ordinary day when you are just minding your own business, not expecting anything, and your desire is just to serve God.

So I'm going to be faithful in my division. I'm going to be faithful at my post. I'm going to be faithful with my assignment. Whatever You ask me to do, that is what I'm going to do. On an ordinary day—maybe at a Tuesday Bible study, maybe a Wednesday men's day, maybe a Thursday Trees of Righteousness, maybe a Friday prayer meeting, maybe a Saturday at choir rehearsal, maybe on a Sunday—the extraordinary happens.

This is why you cannot afford to miss the visitation of God. I hear the invitation to "bring your children out on Friday" or "bring your children out for youth services." Many times parents are too tired, but you don't know the day God is going to break the yoke off the life of your child. You don't know the day God is going to destroy the yoke that has been binding your child for years, and God says extraordinary things happen on an ordinary day.

Stay at your post. I press my way, but I do get tired I'm human like the rest of us; but I press my way because I might receive a revelation. I don't know when God is going to visit me and elevate me or promote me and take me to my next dimension in Him. So I press my way, and I make sure I'm at my post, because the Bible says it came to pass **while** he was serving.

(2) The Altar of Prayer

Key number two is to go to the altar of incense, which is the altar of prayer.

Luke 1:9:

"According to the custom of the priesthood, his lot fell to burn incense when he went into the temple of the Lord."

Please note that he went in. He wasn't loitering out in the parking lot.

Please know this, child of God. If you've come to worship God, then you've come to worship Him. I believe you should give God enough respect to switch off your cell phone and alert everybody who may try to reach you that between this time and that time is your time with God. Why would you give God your *divided* attention? You came to serve God. You came to worship Him. You came to praise Him, but you still have your cell phone on because you're waiting for another call. Well, God said, if you will serve Baal, serve him. If you will serve God, serve God, for how long will you be caught between two opinions? If you are for God, serve God. If you are for others, serve them.

Church folks have the audacity to come to church and not switch off their cell phones, they deem whoever is supposed to call is more important than God. So what does God do when you get sick? He says, "You go call upon that person you were waiting for." When you are out with your girlfriend or your boyfriend, you switch off the cell phone and are unreachable, because you want to give them your undivided attention.

Back in the Old Testament a priest could have the privilege of burning incense once in the holiest of holies in his entire lifetime, or sometimes even never. Therefore, when given the privilege, it was an absolute honor. I truly believe that because Zacharias was so faithful, God gave him the honor at the altar of the holiest of holies. Burning of incense is symbolic of prayer, of physical worship.

Psalm 141:1-2:

1 "Lord, I cry out to You. Make haste to me! Give ear to my voice when I cry out to You. 2Let my prayer be set before You as incense, the lifting up of my hands as the evening sacrifice."

Incense is a sweet-smelling perfume made from frankincense and other oils. A fire would be lit at the altar of incense, and then the oil would be dropped on the fire, which then would turn into smoke. As it burned, the smoke increased and fumigated the closed place, which was the holiest of holies, with the sweet savor that represented the prayers of the priest. God wants us to come to the altar of prayer. In other words, when you are serving God and you believe God to break the bands of barrenness, you've got to come to a place where you are able to go to the altar of prayer and present your prayers before God so your prayers fumigate and saturate the atmosphere.

To illustrate the meaning of *fumigate,* think of the pest control company when they are trying to kill the termites in your house. They cover your building to get ready to fumigate your home. Because it's a closed environment, everything that is in there that can be caught is going to be caught. So the moment those termites smell the fumigation they begin to die and disappear. So God is saying your prayers have to get to a place where they fumigate your environment, and as the environment is fumigated with the presence of God that has come forth as a result of your prayers, everything in you not like Him, has to die.

The reason it is so difficult for the children of God to die to their attitudes, die to their behavior, die to their habits, is that we have never ever released a prayer that has become as thick as incense so it absolutely fumigated the atmosphere. You have to get to a place where your prayer saturates the atmosphere and fumigates it so it's a thick cloud. All you can smell then is the fume or the incense, which is your prayer. You are caught up and surrounded, and the fumes go past your coat into your system and begin to kill, to fumigate the atmosphere so you can die to the flesh. A lot of us are not seeing what God wants to do for us because we have refused to die. We refuse to die to self. We are self-righteous.

In Revelation 8:3-4:

3 "Then another angel, having a golden censer, came and stood at the altar. He was given much incense, that he should offer it with the prayers of all the saints upon the golden altar which was before the throne. 4 And the smoke of the incense, with the prayers of the saints, ascended before God from the angel's hand."

I really want to teach this. If you haven't read my book *Prayer Is the Master Key*, get a copy today. In that book I speak about the principle of the incense and swinging the incense before the altar of God. The term *smoke of the incense* comes from the Greek word *thumiama,* and the Hebrew rendering is a fragrant powder burnt in swinging censors, which is symbolic of the prayers of the saints that are swung before the Lord.

In spite of their barren, unproductive situation Zacharias let his prayers go before God as incense. Even though Zacharias and Elizabeth were of advanced age they kept praying because they understood prayer is the master key, and nothing leaves heaven until something leaves earth. They also understood that delay is not denial and age had nothing to do with the fulfilling of God's promises.

(3) Wait For God's Timing
Point number three: Before you can birth John the Baptist, you must wait for God's timing.

Luke 1:11-13:

11 "Then an angel of the Lord appeared to him, standing on the right side of the altar of incense. 12And when Zacharias saw him, he was troubled, and fear fell upon him. 13But the angel said to him, 'Do not be afraid, Zacharias, for your prayer is heard; and your wife Elizabeth will bear you a son, and you shall call his name John. And you will have joy and gladness, and many will rejoice at his birth.'"

You must wait for God's timing. Please understand. It's never been about your purpose. It's always been about God's purpose. We get frustrated because we think it's about our purpose, but the Bible says it is never about your purpose or my purpose. Everything in the kingdom is about God's purpose. It is to fulfill the purpose of the kingdom of God. Every gift God gives you is for His purpose. Every anointing He gives you is for His purpose. Every grace He gives you is for His purpose. When God gives you a business, it's for His purpose.

Romans 8:28: *And we know that all things work together for good to them that love God, to them who are the called according to **His purpose**.*

Ephesians 1:9: *Having made known unto us the mystery of his will, according to his good pleasure which **He hath purposed in Himself**:*
1:11: *In whom also we have obtained an inheritance, being predestinated according to the **purpose of Him** who worketh all things after the counsel of His own will:*
3:11: *According to the eternal purpose which **He purposed** in Christ Jesus our Lord:*

2 Timothy 1:9: *Who hath saved us, and called us with an holy calling, not according to our works, but according to **His own purpose** and grace, which was given us in Christ Jesus before the world began.*

Remember the tower of Babel in Genesis 11 when they missed the purpose of God. God had to break it down. The timing of God in answering our prayers is more in step with His purposes than with ours.

Proverbs 19:21 (Amp):

"Many plans are in a man's mind, but it is the Lord's purpose for him that will stand"

I believe that one of the reasons Elizabeth was not able to conceive earlier was that the purpose of God was for Mary to be birthed in the earth realm first. Elizabeth had to wait for Mary to be birthed before God could give Elizabeth a child, because the child Elizabeth was to birth would become the forerunner to prepare the way for the child that was to come forth out of the womb of Mary.

God never does anything outside of purpose, which is His original intent. Everything God does, He does for a purpose. Please understand. God is always on time. God is always on schedule. There is never a time when God is not on schedule, because everything has already been orchestrated in eternity to be fulfilled in time.

Galatians 4:4:

"In the fullness of time God sent His Son born of a woman according to the law".

It took four thousand years for God to send the remedy in the person of His Son Jesus Christ, for what Adam and Eve did in the Garden of Eden (Matt 1:17). Everything has to be done according to God's purpose and in God's timing. Elizabeth, who was ordained to carry John the Baptist, the forerunner who was ordained to prepare the way for Jesus, was unable to conceive **I believe**, because Mary had not yet come into the earth realm. When Mary was in position, God showed up and said, "Now, Elizabeth, it's time for Me to open up your womb because the difference between you and Mary has to be six months."

In God's hidden purpose a forerunner would be summoned and sent before the long-awaited Messiah. In the fullness of time God sent His angel, and the angel said to Zacharias, "Your petition has been heard." After all these years, when you thought God had forgotten you, when you thought God was not going to show up, God heard your petition. "Your wife, Elizabeth, shall bear a son. His name shall be called John."

God's timing brought about a divine sense of purpose, provision and promise far greater than Elizabeth and Zacharias had imagined. God's timing brought about and produced a God-ordained powerful ministry that would be used by God to purge a generation and bring them to repentance, causing them to turn away from their wicked ways. They birthed an anointing that would come in the Spirit and the power of Elijah and fulfill the prophecy of Malachi. **Timing and purpose. Gods timing.**

They birthed an anointing that was the voice that cried in the wilderness. The barrenness of Elizabeth represented the barrenness of Israel, and before purpose and perfection would be birthed, preparation through repentance had to be birthed in the person of John the Baptist. They birthed the voice that caused the valleys to be exalted and the mountains and the hills to be brought low. The valleys of pride, valleys of deception, valleys of religion, valleys of tradition—God used them to birth the voice that caused those valleys to be exalted and the mountains to be brought low, the voice that caused every crooked place to be made straight, every crooked attitude, every crooked behavior, every crooked habit. (Isaiah 40)

God moved them to birth the voice, John the Baptist, to cause the crooked to become straight, the voice that made the rough places smooth. **There can never be times of refreshing and revival until there is repentance.**

Elizabeth birthed the voice that drew crowds to the River Jordan, and they cried because the Spirit of repentance drew them. We are trying, however, to draw people with entertainment and all kinds of gimmicks. But the voice that cried in the wilderness, "Repent and be baptized," was the voice Elizabeth brought forth, and many went.

Acts 3:17-18:

17 "Yet now, brethren, I know that you did it in ignorance, as did also your rulers. 18But those things which God foretold by the mouth of all his prophets, that the Christ would suffer, he has thus fulfilled. 19Repent therefore and be converted, that your sins may be blotted out, so that times of refreshing may come from the presence of the Lord, 20and that He may send Jesus Christ, who was preached to you before, 21whom heaven must receive until the time of restoration of all things, which God has spoken by the mouth of all His holy prophets since the world began."

What am I saying? Before refreshing there has to be repentance. Before restoration there has to be a refreshing. God is a God of order, but we've raised up a people who have taken it the wrong way. Everything is being taught backwards. We teach restoration without refreshing. We teach refreshing without repentance, and God is saying you've got it backward. You've got to teach the people to repent first. If you repent, or turn away from, then times of refreshing will come. When times of refreshing come, then restoration will come.

Repentance simply means to change your mind about the way you think about God. Change your mind about the way you think about the world, for if a man be in Christ he is a new creature. Behold, all things are passed away. All things have become new. You can't have one foot in the world and one foot in the church. God says repent. Before perfection can come, before completion can come, before restoration can come, you've got to repent. You've got to turn away from your wicked ways. You've got to turn away from your unrighteous ways. You've got to turn away from lying and cheating, stealing and fornicating, and committing adultery. **Repent**.

You can't keep living the way you've been living and expect God to fulfill Joel 2 whereby He said, "I will restore unto you." There first has to be a repenting. Let the preachers and the priests hide behind the porch with sackcloth and ashes and begin to birth the voice of John the Baptist that cried, **"Repent."**

We are birthing the voice that will challenge the sinner on the street. I don't want him to be my friend. I want his soul to be saved. I don't want him just to be a churchgoer. I want him to have a relationship with God. When you birth the voice that cries in the wilderness, "Prepare thee the way of the Lord, tell the people, **'Repent.'**"

God says Elizabeth was used to birth John because it was the turning of a new day. The season was significant because God was getting ready to bring a new era and a new movement in the earth realm, and there was no way God would bring in that new era until He had cleaned up the mess of the old era.

Please understand. That is why it's important for you to know the times and the seasons. It is important for you to know when it's a voice and not an echo. The only way you can ever be a voice is when you have been back in the wilderness, feeding on locusts and wild honey, and God Himself has impregnated you with a word for your generation.

A true voice is not confused by other voices, because I hear only the voice that has called me out of darkness into His marvelous light. That's the reason I have the boldness to come and face the Pharisees and the Sadducees, the scribes and the religious people, and the traditional people without fear because I come in the spirit and in the power of Elijah in the voice of John the Baptist crying, **"Repent."**

God is saying that before you can birth **perfection and completion** you've got to repent. **Repentance** comes before **refreshing**, and refreshing comes before **restoration**. I'm telling you we must change our minds and turn away; we are at the threshold of the next dimension of God. I don't know about you, but I would not miss it.

Sing, Elizabeth!

Part 9

Mary, the Virgin

1Sing, O barren, thou that didst not bear; break forth into singing, and cry aloud, thou that didst not travail with child: for more are the children of the desolate than the children of the married wife, saith the Lord. 2Enlarge the place of thy tent, and let them stretch forth the curtains of thine habitations: spare not, lengthen thy cords, and strengthen thy stakes; 3for thou shalt break forth on the right hand and on the left; and thy seed shall inherit the Gentiles, and make the desolate cities to be inhabited.—Isaiah 54:1-3

In Luke 1:26-45 the Bible says:

26"Now in the sixth month the angel Gabriel was sent by God to a city of Galilee named Nazareth, 27to a virgin betrothed to a man whose name was Joseph, of the house of David. The virgin's name was Mary. 28And having come in, the angel said to her, 'Rejoice, highly favored one, the Lord is with you; blessed are you among women!' 29But when she saw him she was troubled at his saying, and considered what manner of greeting this was. 30Then the angel said to her, 'Do not be afraid, Mary, for you have found favor with God. 31And behold, you will conceive in your womb and bring forth a Son, and shall call His name Jesus. 32He will be great, and will be called the Son of the Highest; and the Lord God will give Him the throne of His father David. 33And He will reign over the house of Jacob forever, and of His kingdom there will be no end.'34 "Then Mary said to the angel, 'How can this be, since I do not know a man?'35And the angel answered and said to her, 'The Holy Spirit will come upon you, and the power of the Highest will overshadow you; therefore, also, that Holy One who is to be born will be called the Son of God. 36 Now indeed, Elizabeth your relative has also conceived a son in her old age; and this is now the sixth month for her who was called barren. 37For with God nothing will be impossible.'38Then Mary said, 'Behold the maidservant of the Lord! Let it be to me according to your word.' And the angel departed from her. 39 "Now Mary arose in those days and went into the hill country with haste, to a city of Judah, 40and entered the house of Zacharias and greeted Elizabeth. 41And it happened, when Elizabeth heard the greeting of Mary, that the babe leaped in her womb; and Elizabeth was filled with the Holy Spirit. 42Then she spoke out with a loud voice and said, 'Blessed are you among women, and blessed is the fruit of your womb! 43But why is this granted to me, that the mother of my Lord should come to me? 44For indeed, as soon as the voice of your greeting sounded in my ears, the babe leaped in my womb for joy. 45Blessed is she who believed, for there will be a fulfillment of those things which were told her from the Lord.'"

We have discussed six barren wombs that have birthed six kingdom principles. These included the womb of Sarah, who birthed Isaac, which was symbolic of laughter, and we understood that laughter was a symbol of conquest. We examined the womb of Rebekah that God used to bring forth the seed of Jacob, which was symbolic of change and transformation. We talked about the womb of Rachel that God used to bring forth Joseph, which was symbolic of patience and humility and the womb of Manoah's wife that brought forth Samson, which was symbolic of strength. We looked at the womb of Hannah that brought forth Samuel, which means the name of God, which was symbolic of the prophetic. We talked about the womb of Elizabeth that God used to bring forth John the Baptist, which was symbolic of repentance and preparation.

Now we will talk about Mary. The womb of Mary was not a barren womb per say, but it was a virgin womb. It was a womb that was absolutely untouched. It was pure and clean. It was holy. When God was getting ready to come down in the earth realm and become a man, God needed a womb that was untouched. Why? Because God is holy and God is pure.

So Mary, a virgin, was espoused to be married to a man by the name of Joseph. Please understand. The Bible does not speak about dating between young men and women. The Bible speaks about being espoused, whereby you are promised to someone for marriage. You are set aside for someone for marriage. In other words, when someone saw you and liked you, or the family spotted a young woman suitable for their son, they went to that family and asked for the hand of the daughter for their son. If the young woman's family approved it, they set her aside until the fullness of time when they would come forth and she would be taken for a wife.

So there was nothing like dating to see if you were compatible. Either you took it, or you didn't. So the Bible says that Mary was espoused to marry Joseph. Both of them came from very strong spiritual pedigree, and God ordained Mary's womb to carry God in the earth realm.

After you have been changed, after you have been strengthened, after you have been anointed and appointed, there comes a time when God brings you into an arena whereby you come into completion and perfection.

The feast of tabernacles took place in the seventh month, according to Leviticus 23. As we continue to sing, the Lord will conform us to His image and to His likeness. It's time to consider the barrenness of the virgin Mary. She was not barren, *per se*, but because her womb had never been touched, she had never been impregnated, she had never conceived with a seed from a man, she could really be put in the category of barren.

Luke 1:26-27:

26 *"And in the sixth month the angel Gabriel was sent from God unto a city of Galilee, named Nazareth,* 27*to a virgin espoused to a man whose name was Joseph, of the house of David; and the virgin's name was Mary."*

I want you to look at the detail of this particular Scripture passage. The angel was not confused. He came with specific instructions. He knew where he was going. He was not asking for someone to show him where Mary lived. He came already knowing Mary's address. In other words, when you have an assignment on your life God knows where to find you.

Looking at different avenues in the Word of God, God shows us elements about people who were called to greatness. He takes us to examples in the Word of God of people who were ordained to do great things. One of the things that was prevalent among these people is that none of them looked for God. God looked for them.

Looking back to the life of Elisha and Elijah. The Bible says the old prophet Elijah went looking for Elisha, He found him plowing with twelve yokes of oxen, and Elisha was on the twelfth yoke. The Bible says Elijah threw the mantle on Elisha.

Looking at the life of David who was on the back side of the desert, tending the sheep of his father, minding his own business, not looking for anyone, not looking for a title, wasn't looking for any oil on his head, wasn't looking for anything. He was content and happy, doing what he had been called to do.

The Bible says God sent Samuel. He told Samuel to take up the horn of oil and go to the house of Jesse the Bethlehemite and there he would find a king. And Samuel said to his servant "go fetch him"

Looking at the account of Saul when he was to be the next king of Israel. Saul's father had lost his donkeys and couldn't find them, so he sent Saul to find them. When Saul couldn't find them he went to the prophet Samuel who was told by God to anoint Saul as king. But Saul did not want to be king. So, when they went looking for Saul, they said, "He hideth among the stuff."

1 Samuel 10:21-24:

21 When he had caused the tribe of Benjamin to come near by their families, the family of Matri was taken, and Saul the son of Kish was taken: and when they sought him, he could not be found. 22 Therefore they enquired of the LORD further, if the man should yet come thither. And the LORD answered, **Behold, he hath hid himself among the stuff.** *23 And they ran and fetched him thence: and when he stood among the people, he was higher than any of the people from his shoulders and upward. 24 And Samuel said to all the people, See ye him whom the LORD hath chosen, that there is none like him among all the people? And all the people shouted, and said, God save the king.*

When God is ready to place His hand on your life, God knows where to find you. Your gift will make room for you. You don't have to try to make room for your gift (Proverbs 18:16).

When Jesus began His ministry, the Bible says in Luke 4:1 that after He was baptized Jesus was led into the wilderness for forty days and forty nights where He was tempted by Satan. He overcame the three temptations stated in 1 John 2:16, which are

(1) **Lust of the flesh,** Luke 4:2b-4: *he did eat nothing and when they were ended he afterward hungered. And the devil said unto him, if thou be the Son of God, command this stone that it be made bread. And Jesus answered him, saying, It is written, that man shall not live by bread alone, but by every Word of God;*

(2) **Lust of the eye,** vs 5 *And the devil, taking him up into an high mountain, shewed unto him all the kingdoms of the world in a moment of time;*

(3) **Pride of life,** vs 6 (amp) *"and he said to Him, To You I will give all this power and authority and their glory (all the magnificence, excellence, preeminsence, dignity, and grace), for it has been turned over to me, and I give it to whomever I will. 7 Therefore if You will do homage to and worship me*

(just once), it shall be Yours. 8 And Jesus replied to him, get behind Me Satan! It is written, you shall do homage to and worship the Lord your God, and Him only shall you serve.

Jesus passed each and every one of those tests, Luke 4:16 says, *"And He came to Nazareth, where he had been brought up: and as His custom was, he went into the synagogue on the Sabbath day, and stood up for to read.* Luke 4:17 declares, *"There was __delivered unto Him__ the book of the Prophet Esaias."*

He had returned in the power, but He did not ask for the scroll. He did not tell the priest He now had power and He was not the person the priest knew before. He just humbly went and stood up to read, because the book was handed to Him. He had come into the fullness of His purpose. The priest had no choice but to recognize the oil, the anointing and the unction that was on His head, and he gave Him the scroll. The oil will find your head.

You will remember the season of Esther, whereby the crown was seeking for a head because the crown was headless. When Vashti misbehaved before the king, the crown was taken off Vashti, and the crown became headless. Therefore, in a manner of speaking, the crown was looking for another head.

The point here is that when God is getting ready to use you, He knows where to find you. That is why it behooves us not to despise people. It would behoove us not to look down on certain people because the person you look down on is a person God has reserved the right to raise up, elevate and use for His glory. You see, God is no respecter of persons. God is a respecter of principles. Understand— God wants you to position yourself so that when the oil, when the crown, when the scepter is looking for you it will find you.

The Bible says when Jesus began His ministry He began to walk. He went by the river of Galilee where He saw several of the disciples. One by one He found them. He found one casting his net. Jesus said, "Get up and follow Me." And He found the two sons of Zebedee mending their nets, and He said to them, "Get up and follow Me." Jesus found them; they did not find Him.

Mary was positioned; she was chaste; she was a virgin; she was pure. And when the fullness of time came God was looking for a womb that would bring Him into the earth realm. One of the things I respect about God is that God does not break His own law. It is God who ordained that there is one entry point for man in the earth realm, and that is through the womb of a woman. Therefore, God could not break the protocol just because He was God. He had to follow the protocol He had set in motion. "Even though I am God, I must become man and come into the earth realm through the womb of a woman." So Mary was situated for God to use her.

When you speak about the angels of the Lord, they each have a special rank. There are rankings in the angelic realm. Every angel is given a different assignment. Order started in heaven. That is why, when you open your mouth to pray, let it be on earth as it is in heaven (Luke 11:2). You need to be watchful what you're praying, because order is in heaven, and all of the angels were assigned specific tasks. The angel Gabriel was a messenger angel. He was the angel that brought messages from God.

So now Gabriel came to Mary, and the first salutation Gabriel had for Mary was this: "You are blessed and highly favored with God." Before you are able to birth perfection and completion, God wants you to understand you are highly favored of Him. It doesn't matter what it looks like. If God has favored you, there is nothing anyone can do about it.

I heard a preacher say one time that favor is not fair, and if you have God's favor, sometimes people will look at you and wonder how you did what you did or how you got what you got, how you are able to be who you are. And all you have to do is look at them and tell them straight to their face, "I am blessed and highly favored."

The angel assured Mary, "You are favored." The word *favor* comes from the Greek word *eulogeo*. It means you are well thought of; you are well spoken of; you are in good books with God. That was to assure Mary, because a visitation of an angel was not a visitation that happened every single day. In other words, you don't wake up every day expecting an angel to knock at your door; but there you are just doing what you're supposed to do, minding your own business, and all of a sudden the angel of the Lord appears. Of course, when the angel revealed himself to Mary the Bible says she was troubled.

(1) Do Not be Troubled

The first key I want you to remember is that before you are able to birth perfection and completion, do not be troubled. God is not going to birth completion and perfection in your life if you allow your spirit to be agitated and troubled. You have to be able to trust God. Peace is the absence of war. So God wants you to come into a realm and a place where you are not troubled, where you are not agitated, because He is getting ready to deposit something significant, something powerful, something awesome in your womb. Mary was getting ready to carry God.

When we talk about the divine nature, Jesus was very man and very God. As man in **His humanity** Jesus hungered, Jesus laughed, Jesus wept, Jesus was tired, Jesus slept. In **His divinity** Jesus cast out devils Jesus laid hands on the sick, and they recovered, Jesus raised the dead.

God wants us to understand that we are partakers of the divine nature of God (2 Peter 1:4). Within your **humanity** you are carrying **divinity**. When Mary conceived, she received the seed of God. Mary literally received God's Word as the sperm that permitted her womb to conceive and conception to take place, and she was impregnated with God 1 John 3:9 (amp):

*No one born (begotten) of God [deliberately, knowingly, and ᶦhᶦhabitually] practices sin, for God's nature abides in him [His principle of life, the **divine sperm**, remains permanently within him]; and he cannot practice sinning because he is born (begotten) of God.*

You and I are pregnant with God. If you have the Word of God, the Word is God and God is the Word. If the Word is God and if God is the Word, then you are carrying God. That's the reason everything has to move and shift to accommodate you when you have a hundredfold revelation of who you are, but not because of your **humanity**; it's because of the **divinity that lives in you**. There is a divine nature within your humanity.

2Corinthians 4:7:

But we have this **treasure** in earthen vessels, that the excellency of the power may be of God, and not of us.

In His humanity Jesus wept at the death of Lazarus because He loved him. But in his divinity when Jesus went to the tomb of Lazarus he commanded Lazarus to come forth. He didn't weep at the tomb of Lazarus because He switched from His humanity to divinity. He knew what to do, when to do it and how to do it.

The act of Mary birthing perfection and completion is about your understanding that in your **humanity** you are carrying **divinity**. The moment you switch from humanity to divinity every spirit, every power, every principality and every demon become subject to the divine nature that is in you. This thing is weighty, it's powerful. You are carrying salvation; you are carrying healing, you are carrying the deliverance of the nations. You are carrying the power of God that has the ability to destroy every yoke and remove every burden. You are carrying something, and it is a holy thing.

Even Gabriel couldn't give it a name, He just called it a thing. Because it was so divine and within Gods plan of redemption for man according to

Genesis 3:15:

...*that the seed of the woman would bruise the head of the serpent.*

It was hidden even from the celestial beings. In other words, whatever you want that thing to become is what it will become. If you wanted it to become a deliverer, it became a deliverer. If you wanted it to be a savior, it became a savior. If you wanted it to be a healer, it became a healer.

I understand the importance of giving you keys and points, but I do want you to get the revelation of this point. I want you to get the thrust of it and go away with a fresh understanding that the whole purpose and the whole concept are that as you begin to walk in the earth realm you become the Living Word.

In other words, you become Jesus in the earth realm, and in the same way Jesus walked you begin to walk because you are carrying something holy.

One of the reasons the innkeepers were not able to be partakers of the blessing Mary was carrying was because there was no room in the inns.

Luke 2:7:

And she brought forth her firstborn son, and wrapped him in swaddling clothes, and laid him in a manger; because there was no room for them in the inn.

Joseph took Mary and went to Nazareth because it was the time for paying their taxes. The Bible says that when they got there they were looking for a place where Mary could give birth. They went from door to door, but there was no room in the inns and the innkeepers did not endeavor to make room perhaps because they had no perception of what Mary was carrying. Every inn they went to shut the door on them, but the innkeepers didn't realize that every time they shut the door, they shut the door on their deliverance, healing and salvation of the world, Jesus Christ the son of God.

Matthew 1:21:

And she shall bring forth a son, and thou shalt call his name JESUS: for He shall save his people from their sins.

Luke 1:31-32:

And behold, thou shalt conceive in thy womb, and bring forth son, and shalt call his name JESUS. He shall be great, and shall be called the Son of the Highest: and the Lord God shall give unto him the throne of His Father David.

Perhaps if they had known what she was carrying, they would have made room. We are a type of the inn and the bible says in.

Revelations 3:20:

Behold, I stand at the door and knock: if any man hear my voice and open the door, I will come in to him, and will sup with him, and he with Me.

Have you made room for Him, if you have not why don't you open the door of your heart and make room for the King of kings and Lord of lords.

Do you know what you are carrying? Please understand that when you have a revelation of this, you will never be intimidated. You can never let any demon intimidate you because you know what you're carrying and because you know at any moment, in any season, all you have to do is make the switch from **humanity to divinity.**

Don't be fooled by the look. You can't tell who I am just by looking at me, but there's something in me, something in my spirit. There is power; an anointing. It is not about the outward appearance but about what I'm carrying on the inside. I could be talking to you right now in my humanity; but when I switch into the divine, then all of a sudden I become the voice of God and tell you the matters of your heart.

(2) Receive the Impossible

Key number two is to believe, and you shall receive the impossible. The Bible says Mary heard the announcement that she was about to conceive. In other words, she may not have fully understood it, but she was just going to believe it.

Mary didn't fully understand it. She asked how these things could be since she knew not a man. She was a virgin. Her womb had never been touched. She was chaste, closed and pure. The meaning of *virgin* is one who has never been touched, a woman who has never had sexual intercourse with a man, or a marriageable maiden, a virtuous one. It means a man who has abstained from all uncleanness and whoredom and has kept his chastity, a man who has never had intercourse with a woman. So please understand the word *virgin* does not refer only to women; it's for men too.

The Bible says to believe and you will receive the impossible. No word of God is void of power. Every word of God has power. He spoke His word, and the word performed the purpose to which it was sent. Once the word of God was released to Mary, the word set in motion a divine plan and activated her womb; and thus her womb opened up and conceived.

(3) Go up to the high places

The Bible says Mary went to the high places, which means the heavenlies. Before you and I can birth perfection and completion, we must be able to go to the heavenlies. The Bible says, *"And He raised us up together with Him and made us sit down together (giving us joint seating with Him) in the heavenly sphere (by virtue of our being) in Christ Jesus (The Messiah, the Anointed One)* (Ephesians 2:6 *Amp*). *Heavenly* refers to a realm, a dimension. There is a place, where God requires you and me to come to through prayer, praise and worship. As we pray and as we worship, we climb higher and higher until we are seated with Him in heavenly places. The Bible says it is the place called *Above All* whereby you are seated above all principalities, powers, dominions, thrones. Nothing can touch you when you get to that place called *Above All*.

Eph 1:20-21:

"Which he wrought in Christ, when He raised Him from the dead, and set Him at His own right hand in the heavenly places, 21 Far above all principality, and power, and might and dominion, and every name that is named, not only in this world, but also in that which is to come"

(4) Enter in

The Bible says she entered a city. All the cities had gates, and Mary could have gone to the gates of the city but not entered in, but the Bible says she **entered in**.

Psalm 100:

"I will enter His gates with thanksgiving and I will enter His courts with praise."

In other words, a lot of people are not able to birth completion and perfection because they get to the gate of Judah but never enter in.

Judah means praise. Many people come to the gates of praise, but they never enter into the city of praise. There will be singing and clapping in a service, and the praise and worship leader is saying, "Clap your hands, lift your hands and praise the Lord," but you just sit there at the gate. If you never lift your hands or open your mouth and be a part of the worship service, or if you never sing and pray and give accolades to God with all the glory and all the honor, then you are at the gate, but you've never entered the city.

The Bible says Mary entered into the city of Judah. In other words, Judah is a city; praise is a city. It has borders; it has boundaries; it has gates. So you come, but you stop at the outer court of Judah. That's where everybody is doing anything. That's where the dogs are, where the filth is. But the Bible says that after leaving the outer court you enter the inner court. Before you go into the inner court you go by the altar whereby you've got to wash and be clean because you are dirty. You've got to sanctify yourself, but because many of us don't want to wash off our filth we choose to stay at the gate and never enter into the city of Judah.

I can do a whole teaching on Judah alone or a seven-week teaching on praise, because praise has levels and dimensions. There's no way you can begin to walk in the fullness of praise until you understand the birthing of praise. It's elementary praise when you try to show off what God has done, just to prove God has blessed you.

Praise has to grow. It has to come from the place of being an infant to become a mature man. When your praise grows, then your focus changes, and then you are not praising God just because you are trying to impress someone. You are praising God because you have a relationship with God. You have to be able to take praise to a whole new dimension.

The Bible says in Genesis 49 that Jacob called his sons and began to bless each of them. Jacob had become Israel, and when he blessed Judah, Judah was an old man. It was not that type of elementary Judah who had no sense. It was a Judah who had matured, a Judah who had grown, and now his father blessed him and said, "Judah, you are a lion's whelp. Your eyes shall be red as wine, and your hand will be in the neck of your enemy." In other words, when your praise comes to maturity, your praise is no longer just something you do because you've got to do it. Your praise becomes a weapon.

Let the high praises of God be in your mouth and the two-edged sword in your hand to execute vengeance. (Psalm 149:6-7) When I open my mouth, I'm not praising to impress you. I'm praising because I have my foot on the neck of a demon. I have my foot on the neck of some spirit that is trying to intimidate and infiltrate my family, my home, my children. Then my praise becomes a weapon of warfare, and I squeeze the life out of the enemy.

That's the reason you cannot afford to let people interfere with your praise. I'm talking about mature praise, because everything they are doing has a purpose. When they begin to praise and they get to a certain place, they are praising God with everything that is within them. Their hands move, and their feet move, because they are in warfare in the realm of the Spirit and their praise has become warfare. They are cutting down something in the realm of the Spirit.

People of God, there was a time when Judah was besieged under the kingship of Jehoshaphat. Three nations came against Judah. The Bible says Jehoshaphat feared, and he called a solemn fast. That's the first thing you do when fear hits you. You'd better ask for some supernatural strength. You can't do it by yourself; you need God's help.

The Bible says that when Jehoshaphat called a solemn fast the whole of Judah fasted. The king had called the fast, but the Spirit of the Lord gave the answer through a young man by the name of Jahaziel. The Spirit fell upon Jahaziel, and God began to speak through him. Jahaziel then gave King Jehoshaphat the answer and the strategy for the enemy that had come against him.

2 Chronicles 20:15:

"Listen, all you of Judah and you inhabitants of Jerusalem, and you, King Jehoshaphat! Thus says the Lord to you: 'Do not be afraid nor dismayed because of this great multitude, for the battle is not yours, but God's.'"

Now when they gave him the assurance, his strength returned and when the strength returned he told the men of Judah to gather their weapons and get ready because God was going to fight for them. God then gave further instruction. He said, "You're not going to fight the way you think you're going to fight, because the weapons you are trying to use are not the weapons that are going to accomplish the victory." He said, "Wake up early tomorrow, and all you have to do is do what your name represents. If your name is Judah, then you will fight the battle with Judah. If your name is praise, then you will fight the battle with praise."

The Bible says they woke up the following morning and began to praise God with every instrument, and as they praised God the enemies became confused. God then set an ambush for the enemies. When you understand the maturity of praise and begin to praise God, God sets an ambush for your enemy, and the enemy gets confused. The enemy will think you are coming one way, only to realize you are coming from the other way. Praise has the power to confuse the enemy and set an ambush for every enemy.

Attending church is not about being a spectator but a participator, while you sit at the gates and everyone else has entered in. One day you'll be asking God why your breakthrough has not come. God will say you're not going to get a breakthrough at the gates. You get your breakthrough when you enter in. I know entering in takes effort, and that's why you have to break off everything that interferes with entering in. That is why when the congregation enters into the worship and praise service, it is not good for you to show up late and interrupt someone who is trying to enter in. But because you don't have discernment, you are interrupting someone who may be on the brink of entering in. When you break that process it will be very difficult for that person to get back to that place again.

That's why I tell the people that when I'm worshiping they should never touch me. They can just sit still and wait. There is nothing more important to me at that point in time than touching the heart of God. Nothing.

The Bible says that when Mary saw the angel she was troubled at his saying as to what manner of salutation this should be. The word *troubled* here means to be agitated greatly, through and through. This is the lot of those who follow the lamb all the way, singing as they go. She was cast in her mind, or she was reasoning through, this strange announcement. Hers was to be the vessel through which God in the flesh was to be manifested. This had never happened before in the manner the Lord now chose. So there was a day in the earth of an unprecedented call of God upon His people. We have not passed this way before, and we have not heard this word before. God is saying, "Prepare your spirit to be a carrier of God."

Luke 1:31-33:

31 "And, behold, thou shalt conceive in thy womb, and bring forth a son, and shalt call his name Jesus. 32He shall be great, and shall be called the Son of the Highest: and the Lord God shall give unto him the throne of his father David: 33And he shall reign over the house of Jacob for ever; and of his kingdom there shall be no end."

The name *Jesus* means Jehovah, our salvation, or Jehovah saves. The new birth is the beginning of our salvation. Our spirit has been saved, our soul is being saved, and our body shall be saved. We are delivered (Past), we are being delivered (Now), and we shall be delivered again (Future).

2 Corinthians 1:10:

*"Who **delivered** us from so great a death, and **doth deliver**: in whom we trust that he **will yet deliver** us."*

184

The only thing that gets saved is your spirit. Then everything else—your soul (your will, intellect and emotions) and your flesh—is a process you and I have to work out.

Romans 12:1:

"I beseech thee therefore, brethren, by the mercies of God, that ye present your body a living sacrifice, holy, acceptable unto God, which is your reasonable service."

Romans 7:24:

"O wretched man that I am! Who shall deliver me from the body of this death?"

So when Jesus came He came to destroy death. He removed the sting of death and overcame the last enemy which is death that is found in our flesh.

Mary asked the question, "How shall this be, seeing I know not a man?"

Luke 1:35: *"And the angel answered and said unto her, The Holy Ghost shall come upon thee, and the power of the Highest shall overshadow thee: therefore also that holy thing which shall be born of thee shall be called the Son of God."*

Many of us have been asking this same question. God has visited you on several occasions. God has spoken a word into your spirit. God has given you an indication to be a carrier of His Son, and the answer has always been, "How shall these things be since I know not?"

This is the excuse of the church and the excuse of every generation. How can I do it since I don't have an education? How can I do it since I'm illiterate? How can I do it since I've never gone to seminary? How can I do it?

God is saying, **"The Holy Ghost."**

You may never have gone to a seminary in your life, but if you say yes to God He will take you through the seminary of the Holy Ghost. He will train you through the university of the Holy Spirit. People ask me if I do what I do because I went to Bible college. I tell them it's true, but not true. I went to Bible college, yes. I was taught many things. I was taught the ethics of ministry. I was taught how to exegesis, homiletics, and hermeneutics, I was taught Hebrew, Greek, all of it. But I remember one thing my principal said to us when we graduated. He said, "You have come to Bible college, and you have learned how to put together a three-point sermon, a conclusion and a challenge. You've learned all of that, but my final word to you as you leave the halls of this college is this. If you never use any of the principles you learned here, follow the Holy Ghost." That comment never left me.

Everything we learned there was just structure. It was just guidelines, but the ultimate teacher for our entire season of ministry will be God, the Holy Spirit. I guarantee you that a lot of what I teach I never learned at Bible college. I don't even remember what they taught me in Bible college, if I can be candid with you. I know the basics; I know disciplines; I know ethics; I know submission; I know all that. But when you are talking about the nitty-gritty, the meat of the Word of God, the hundredfold revelation, the things that are deeper than black ink on white paper, I did not learn those in Bible college. The Holy Ghost has been my teacher.

Every time I study the Word of God, every time I go to the Word and seek the face of God, I ask God, "Holy Spirit, my senior partner, my Paraclete, my best friend, come and teach me. Come and illuminate God's Word. Open the Scripture and reveal it to me. Take me deeper and show me what God is really saying." Suddenly the light of the Holy Spirit will take one little verse and blow it up, and it blows my mind.

It's wonderful for us to read books and buy tapes, but the greatest teacher is the Holy Spirit, the holy thing that lives inside us. If I lost all my books, my computer and my laptop and didn't have any of that I would still be able to stand up and preach for three hours, because the Holy Ghost is locked in my spirit.

I will never forget the time we were going to Maryland on a red-eye flight. We were all tired, and out of everything they picked up they forgot my briefcase with all my notes in it for my message. So we arrived in Maryland with big suit carriers with dresses and suits and shoes, but no little briefcase. So as they were trying to find it I just went into my room, and I said, "Well, Holy Ghost, it's on tonight. It's going to be just you and me preaching."

We went in there that night, and I had no notes or anything but the holy thing in me. The Holy Ghost blew in that place like a tornado, hallelujah! The Holy Ghost will overshadow you. God has sent His angel, according to Galatians 4:13-14, to visit the woman, which is the church. She is a habitation of purity and will bring forth the Christ in corporate fullness, as seen also in 1 Corinthians 13:8-13.

Sing, Mary. Break forth and cry, for no word of God shall be void of power. There shall be conformity in the song and in its fruit. In Psalm 103:1-2:

> *1 "Bless the Lord, O my soul: and all that is within me, bless his holy name. 2Bless the Lord, O my soul, and forget not all his benefits."*

You will bring forth seven wonderful kinds of fruit. It will take time to grow some of that fruit, but I want to give you seven immediate results of singing unto the Lord.

1. The fruit of visitation. God will visit you; Job 36:27
2. The fruit of transformation; Psalm 115:8; 2 Corinthians 3:8
3. The fruit of revelation; 1 Samuel 3:1-10
4. The fruit of communication; Ephesians 4:15; Psalm 29
5. The fruit of purification; Proverbs 27:21; Psalm 22:3; Malachi 3
6. The fruit of realization of victory; 2 Chronicles 20; Psalm 149
7. The fruit of multiplication; 1 Peter 2:9-10; Isaiah 60:1

Everywhere you go these days you can hear the church singing. Sarah has come out of her tent. Rebekah has jumped off her camel.

Rachel has done away with her teraphim [Idles] Manoah's wife is speaking up. Hannah's sigh has become a song. Something in the womb of Elizabeth is leaping. Mary has believed and received the impossible.

Laughter is the heir of God. The sun has risen upon Peniel Gen 32:31. Every one of us must experience Peniel. Peniel is the place where Jacob had an encounter with God (Gen 32:24-29) that changed his life forever. Gen 32:30 *"And Jacob called the name of the place Peniel: for I have seen God face to face, and my life is preserved,"* it is the place where your life is spared and not snatched away. Peniel is the place of transformation

Gen 32:28:

"And he said, Thy name shall be called no more Jacob (swindler, thief, supplanter)*, but Israel: for as a prince hast thou power with God and with men, and hast prevailed."* The spirit of patience and humility likewise are being unveiled in the eyes of the brethren.

Strength is about to smite the laws of the Philistines. Repentance and purging are gathering a crowd on the banks of baptism. Most important, Jesus, who is total perfection, the completion and fulfillment of all things, the pattern, the Son, our Savior and Lord, is coming forth in all His glory and splendor. He has come, He is coming, and He shall come. Arise, O barren, and sing to your King.

Arise and sing. The song causes the darkness to disburse. The song challenges the powers of darkness and threatens your enemy. Sing, O barren, thou that didst not bear. God wants you to know you are going to bring forth many. Your song is going to change.

Psalm 40:

"I waited patiently for the Lord, and He heard my cry. And he brought me out of a horrible pit. But the Lord has given me a new song, and all shall see it."

The question is, How do you see what is meant to be heard? When you sing they hear the song, when a song is sung, it is meant to be heard and not seen In other words, there will be a **manifestation of those things that have been promised. When preparation meets purpose there is a performance, and there shall be a performance of those things that were spoken.**

God has spoken.

Numbers 23:19:

"God is not a man that He should lie, neither the son of man that He should repent. Hath he said, and shall he not do it? Or hath he spoken, and shall he not make it good" Yes He will!

Psalm 33:9:

"for He spake, and it was done; He commanded, and it stood fast."

Sing, O barren!

Contat Us

For More information regarding
Pastor Sarah Morgan, Women of Vision
or to order products from the ministry
Please log on to our website at
www.womenofvisionla.org or call our
Women of Vision Hotline:
1-888-846-4846
310-672-1500
or write us at:
Women of Vision
P.O. Box 361074
Los Angeles, CA. 90036

Printed in the United States
110746LV00002B/157-999/P

9 781604 777109